GIOVANNI POLIZZI

COMPENDIUM OF

THEORY, METHODOLOGY, AND TECHNIQUE OF

N E G O T I A T I O N

Compendium of Theory, Methodology, and Technique of Negotiation
Copyright © 2021 Giovanni Polizzi
All rights reserved.
ISBN: 978-1-716-08442-3

CONTENTS

Part Three: TECHNIQUE OF NEGOTIATION

Introduction

About thirty years ago, those who in Italy questioned any database with the keyword *negotiator* would find nothing more than the title of a good novel by Frederick Forsyth, *The Negotiator*, translated and published in 1989 by Mondadori. The same term would reappear nine years later also as the title of a film, a fascinating 1998 action thriller starring Samuel Jackson and Kevin Spacey, *The Negotiator*, which, however, with Forsyth's novel shared only the title. As for dictionaries, the excellent Devoto&Oli's *Dictionary of the Italian Language*, confirming the meaning dictated by common sense, defined as negotiator "the one who actively participates in trade or, more often, diplomatic negotiations" and as negotiation "the bargaining for the conclusion of a contract or a diplomatic agreement".

Today, a rapid search on the Internet is enough to come across, in Italy as in other countries, a myriad of writings of all kinds on negotiation, some of them more or less approximate, partial or disorganized, others more or less inspired by the few and valid classics of American literature on the subject, and therefore very similar to each other. What is more, multimedia platforms also offer a wide, but uneven, choice of videos and video clips, which draw inspiration from the multiple problems of negotiation and try to provide visual examples and practical suggestions, which are more or less useful or fun.

The reality is that a subject, whose origins do not go back beyond the last sixty years, born and developed in the context of modern theories on management and the business sciences developed by Anglo-American literature, has so far found no suitable space for reflection either in a more European culture or tradition of academic research, due to the absolute pre-eminence of the American school and vice versa, in Europe, the small number of scholars, chairs or university courses dedicated to it.

This Compendium intends to help remedy this shortcoming. It consists of three parts, respectively dedicated to the "theory", "methodology", and "technique" of negotiation. The first part, after a brief excursus on the historical developments of the discipline, intends to set out the main contents of the subject, clearly defining notions, basic concepts, and institutes of both negotiation and conflict (which is usually a potential premise of the former). The second aims to identify, on the basis of the most widespread and established methods, an original methodology of approach useful to the "good negotiator", both national and international, also with a view to a sought-after "culture of negotiation". Finally, the third aims, for a better understanding of the arduous path from conflict to consensus, to frame everything in the concrete context of a standard negotiation process and its different phases, illustrating its fundamental aspects and operational contents and each time providing the reader with the necessary indications and those considered most useful.

It should also be noted that, while "technique" of negotiation (as a trend, attitude or particular mode of action) is an ancient "art" born with the rise of human beings and with their socialization, "theory" and "methodology", as mentioned above, are much less so. Since the study of negotiation is also an interdisciplinary subject, as we will see, strongly influenced by contributions from other disciplines, it is not easy to identify its most remote origins unless by convention or to define its development and orientation, in literature and doctrine, independently of those of other subjects interconnected with it.

Part One

THEORY OF NEGOTIATION

1.1. Origins and developments

In a broad sense, and beyond the philosophical-moral or politico-military teachings of classical antiquity (among which we can include some famous Oriental texts[1]), the first hints of a discipline of negotiation can be identified for some, albeit limited, aspects in the so-called humanistic-pedagogical literature of the 16th and 17th centuries. Texts such as *Il Principe (The Prince)* by Niccolò Machiavelli (1513), *Il Cortegiano* (*The Courtier*) by Baldassarre Castiglione (1528), *De Civilitate morum puerilium* (*A Handbook on Good Manners for Children*) by Erasmus of Rotterdam (1530), or the *Galateo (The Rules of Polite Behavior)* by Monsignor Giovanni Della Casa (1558), containing rules of behaviour and good manners, advice on cunning and wisdom, and tactics of self-control and dissimulation to favour the social advancement of those trying to access the areas of power or enter the court, can be considered among the first to represent some systematic treatment of the best way to manage interpersonal relationships and conflict situations.

The history of diplomacy also gives us an interesting example of how, at the time, it was understood as negotiating activity especially that of diplomats themselves.

Bernardo Navarro, Ambassador of the "Serenissima" to the Papal Court in 1558, wrote in fact in one of his reports to the Venetian Senate for the Doge: "I have learned, Serenissimo Principe, in the Legations in which for many years your Serenity liked to use me, that the Ambassador's office is divided into three parts: in understanding and warning, in which diligence is necessary; *in negotiating, in which it admirably benefits dexterity*; and in

[1] The oldest of which seems to have been the Chinese text *Guiguzi*, a philosophical treatise attributed to a legendary master of the same name who lived in the 5th century B.C. who, borrowing principles from Confucianism and Taoism, perhaps first dealt with issues related to communication, psychology and negotiation in social relations and political struggle.

reporting, where judgment matters so much, talking about the necessary and useful things, and leaving vain and useless". And against the trend he added, with that cultural and moral depth that marked the greatness of Venetian diplomacy: "which three parts are certainly incomplete if they are not treated with faith".

However, it was not until the beginning of the 18th century that *negotiation* appears for the first time in the title of a book dedicated to it, which is therefore conventionally considered as the first official text on the subject. It is no coincidence that this is the work of a diplomat, François De Callières (1645-1717) from France, entitled *De la manière de négocier avec les souvereins*, and published in Paris in 1716[2]. Starting from the assumption that "the very fate of states often depends on the way in which negotiations are conducted and therefore on the ability of the negotiators", the author draws up a detailed repertoire of rules of conduct of the good negotiator, focusing in particular on the importance of knowing the history and culture of the counterparty and on the need for discipline and self-control, but also on the usefulness of showing oneself to be honest and in good faith ("the negotiator must guard against appearing as an excessively skilled or cunning manipulator").

It would be another sixty-two years before negotiation returns as the title of another author's writing. At the height of Enlightenment Encyclopedism, the Italian Fortunato Bartolomeo De Felice (1723-1789) published in French the text *Des négociations, ou de l'art de négocier*[3], which appeared in 1778 simultaneously for the

---

[2] In addition to its first edition in French (M. Brunet, Paris, 1716), the text can also be found on the web, and in English translation in A.F. Whyte, *On the Manner of Negotiating with Princes*, University of Notre Dame Press, 1963, or in H.M.A. Keens-Soper and K.W. Schweizer (edited by), *The Art of Diplomacy*, Leicester University Press, 1983.

[3] F.B. De Félice, *Des négociations, ou de l'art de négocier*, In *Dictionnaire de justice naturelle et civile: code de l'Humanité, ou la Législation universelle, naturelle, civile et politique comprise par une société de gens de lettres et mise en ordre alphabétique par De Félice* (Yverdun),

printing-presses of the Universities of Naples and Bern (where the author had taken refuge from Naples due to unfortunate personal events). As De Callières seems to have preceded the current concept of *intercultural communication*, so De Felice seems to anticipate that of *interdependence* ("It is only in modern Europe, where the inhabitants are united by similar customs, a common religious base, frequent trade and continuous intellectual communication, that negotiation has become the rank of art and has established itself"). The attention to the psychological aspect of negotiation is more lucid and aware in him than in his predecessor. While reiterating the ever-necessary self-control, De Felice realistically dwells on the impossibility of eliminating emotions altogether (also "because it would be dangerous to be completely deprived of them") and therefore on the inevitable role that they assume in any negotiating situation.

The philosophical-literary Romanticism of the 19th century did not promote further theoretical reflections on negotiation, but produced a vast number of historical-diplomatic examples culminating in the Treaties that ended the First World War. A rare exception, though inspired by dialectics and not by a (still non-existent) theory of negotiation, was Arthur Schopenhauer's (1788–1860) short treatise *Eristische Dialektik oder Die Kunst, Recht zu behalten, in 38 Kunstgriffen dargestellt* (*The Art of Being Right: 38 Ways to Win an Argument*)[4], in which the philosopher provides 38 tricks, legal and illegal, to be used to be proved right: to defend it when you are right, and to be right even when right is on the side of the opponent.

University of Naples and Bern, 1778; in English version, *Negotiations, or the Art of Negotiating*, in W. Zartman, *The 50% Solution*, Anchor Press, New York, 1976.

[4] Written in Berlin in 1830-31, published posthumously under the title *Dialektik* by Brockhaus, Leipzig, 1864, the text belongs to *Manuscript Remains in Four Volumes*, Vol. III, "Berlin Manuscripts (1818-1830)," Berg, Oxford/New York/Munich, 1989, also published, under this German title, by Haffmans, Zurich, 1983.

The universalist fervour born of the ashes of the Great War and the hopes of a world from which every conflict was banished slowly sprouted what then, in the middle of the 1930s, and in the wake of the renewed post-Depression spirit of solidarity, took the name of "*Human Relations Movement*". Founded in 1933 by American Elton Mayo[5], who moved from the key idea that 85% of financial success is due to skill in human engineering, to personality and the ability to lead people, the movement had its best-known exponent in Dale Carnegie, of whom we will talk later, whose book *How to Win Friends and Influence People* (1936), although it never mentions negotiation, marked the beginning of the continuing dominance of American literature over the subject in question.

It is precisely in the United States, in fact, from the new post-war climate aiming at economic reconstruction and, in the middle of the Cold War, at a better understanding of the causes of conflicts that the first studies were born on *leadership*[6], conflict itself[7], analysis of decisions, and so-called "*participatory management*"[8]. The progressive spread of these guidelines in Europe also gave rise to the emergence of business sciences, from which the theory of negotiation developed new food for thought, especially for its economic contents. The main interpreters of these guidelines were the two renowned scholars Luce and Raiffa, with their analysis of the well-known *game theory*[9]. The development of this theory applied to negotiation has led other negotiation scholars

---

[5] Elton Mayo, *The Human Problems of an Industrial Civilization*, McMillan, New York, 1933.

[6] E.A. Fleischman, E.F. Harris and H.E. Burtt, *Leadership and Supervision in Industry*, Columbus, Ohio, Bureau of Educational Research, Ohio State University, 1955.

[7] Lewis Alfred Coser, *The Functions of Social Conflict*, Glencoe, Illinois, The Free Press, 1956.

[8] Rensis Likert, *New Patterns of Management*, McGraw-Hill, New York, 1961.

[9] Robert Duncan Luce and Howard Raiffa, *Games and Decisions*, Wiley, New York, 1957.

to integrate it into their research[10], borrowing models and concepts such as, for example, that of the *prisoner's dilemma,* reformulated as the *negotiator's dilemma.*

Since the 1990s, the interest aroused on both sides of the Atlantic by issues and problems related to negotiation, not only among specialists but also among a larger and larger audience, has produced an increasing number of writings on the subject. Some authors have attempted to classify them. Dutchman Mastenbroek's classification[11], although dated, still seems to summarize well the complex panorama of the literature on negotiation, which according to the author can be divided into three main "schools":

a) the first inspired by practical application, to which belong many publications in a *how-to-do-it* style, which are likely to arouse curiosity for their ease of reading and the petty rules of behavioural psychology;

b) the second devoted to studies of specific cases of negotiation, mainly drawn from politics and diplomacy;

c) the last characterized by a more scientific approach, which in turn is linked to two concepts:

c1) one focused on detailed empirical analyses of certain aspects of negotiating activity;

c2) the other devoted to attempts to develop real general theories on negotiation.

The growth of interest in the problems of conflict and negotiation over the last thirty years has also been reflected in the flourishing, first (as always) in America then progressively also in Europe, of study centres, schools and specialized courses. Standing out among all of these is the academic and operational activity carried out at Harvard University, the first major research centre

---

[10] Otomar J. Bartos, *Process and Outcomes of Negotiations*, Columbia University Press, New York, 1974.

[11] Willem Mastenbroek, *Onderhandelen*, Spectrum Uitgeverij Het, Amsterdam, 1984.

on the subject, by the authoritative *Conflict Management Group* (CMG), an international non-profit consulting firm founded in 1984 by Roger Fisher and made up largely of experts and scholars from the *Harvard Law School* (and the connected *Harvard Negotiation Project*, with its *Program on Negotiation-PON*) and other institutions. The CMG, financed with public (including international) and private contributions, provides training and advice for crisis management and negotiated resolution of political, economic, and social conflicts. Its experts have been, and still are, used by governments, large companies, trade unions, and non-governmental organizations.

Finally, with regard to Europe, concrete studies and applications on negotiation have been developed, first, around specific specialization centres, such as the *Laboratoire de Négociation* in Lille or the *Holland Consulting Group* in Amsterdam; then, in general, by international, governmental, and non-governmental organizations, dedicated to conflict prevention and management (such as the *Centre for Humanitarian Dialogue* in Geneva); or on courses at public or private universities (such as, in Italy, the former degree course in International and Diplomatic Sciences at the Gorizia site of the University of Trieste, Bocconi in Milan, LUISS Guido Carli in Rome or the Scuola Superiore Sant'Anna in Pisa), management courses, business administration schools, or study associations on arbitration and mediation.

1.2. Our approach

Negotiation is a phenomenon that must be observed from different angles. Therefore, recent and innovative study, as mentioned, is of a structurally interdisciplinary and composite subject. It contains contributions from different disciplines: from law and contract to the history of treaties and diplomacy; from anthropology to intercultural communication; from mathematical economics to the sciences of organization; from sociology and conflict and peace studies to cognitive, behavioural and language psychology; from semiotics to communication sciences, with particular regard to argumentative analysis, or today to widespread so-called "neuro-linguistic programming".

So why a specific subject such as "Theory, Methodology, and Technique of Negotiation"? First of all, because negotiating activity has always characterized human beings as well as their economic or social activity: next to the "*homo economicus*" or to the "*social animal*" there is therefore in the human being also the nature of a "*negotiator*", which deserves to be analysed and studied in the same way. Furthermore, because negotiation is the most useful instrument for achieving our interests where they depend on others and the most effective means of peaceful resolution of disputes and conflicts of all kinds.

But is any conflict really negotiable? Apparently not, but something is always possible to do[12]. The Romans said that to reach an agreement not only the "*voluntas negotiandi*" (will to negotiate) is necessary but also the "*voluntas concludendi*" (will to conclude). So, what to do if either of these two is missing? When

[12] A well-known English author among negotiating scholars, Gavin Kennedy, published in 1982 (1st edition: Century Hutchinson, London) a book with a significant title *Everything is Negotiable! How to Get the Best Deal Every Time.* The cornerstone of his thinking is that "if we assume that nothing is negotiable unless the other side gives us a different indication, we are missing the opportunity to make better deals for ourselves and the people we deal with."

is it worth negotiating and when not? How can we reach a satisfactory and lasting understanding? What kind of negotiations could we conduct with those who do not share, indeed fight and want to destroy, our system of values? What similarities can there be between negotiations on family issues and negotiations on nuclear disarmament? How can we act in the face of overpowering, brute force, or gratuitous violence? Or finally, how to negotiate (one does not wonder if it is lawful, but only if technically possible) with terrorists and common criminals?

We will try to answer these and other questions, inspired also by the purpose of promoting the spread of a real "culture of negotiation", as a mental habit and useful, intellectual, psychological, and behavioural approach methodology, to the countless situations of clash of interests and interpersonal conflict present in daily life and in the most diverse professional fields.

1.3. Negotiation: phenomenology, notion, and its constituent elements

We all are always negotiating every day, from when we wake up to when we go to sleep, and most of the time without realizing it. We negotiate with our wives, husbands and children, with the retailer on the street corner, with superiors and colleagues or collaborators and employees in the workplace, we negotiate with all sorts of external interlocutors in business or profession, we negotiate (and perhaps it is the most difficult negotiation) even with ourselves!

We have already said that, although the theory and methodology of negotiation are much more recent, the technique of negotiation is instead an ancient "art", since the tendency to negotiate is instinctive and inherent in human beings, born of socialization and communicative interaction with others (the so-called "negotiation with oneself" is not a "negotiation" in the technical sense, but a decision-making process based on alternative choices). From a philosophical point of view, it can therefore be argued that negotiation is a real "category" of human action, since it is innate only in human beings (animals do not negotiate).

As economic science teaches us, every human being who operates rationally always aims to seek profit, that is, to satisfy an extreme variety of needs (and, consequently, interests): where for "*need*" we can understand "the desire to have a reputed means of ending a painful feeling, or preventing it, or to preserve a pleasant feeling, or to provoke it" (according to a beautiful definition by the great economist Maffeo Pantaleoni[13]). Any negotiations, even the non-technical negotiation with oneself, arises from a state of "necessity" that produces, or already coexists with, a situation of actual or potential, inner or external, "conflict": inner (called

[13] Maffeo Pantaleoni, *Principi di Economia Pura (Principles of Pure Economics)*, Barbera, Florence, 1889, reprint by Treves, Milan, 1931.

"intra-personal") conflict is perceived when we find ourselves having to make alternative choices; external (called "inter-personal") conflict is when it is necessary to interact with another subject (and here we approach the technical concept of "negotiation"), to obtain from the same something material or immaterial that we need (a good, an authorization, a consensus, etc., or even a more advantageous form of cooperation).

In these cases of interaction required to resolve an actual or potential conflict, recourse to negotiation is mandatory and inescapable, unless:

a) you are able, and consider it advantageous to do so, to impose on the other your will and your choices (which is difficult and risky, potentially counterproductive, and in any case always expensive in terms of means and energy);

b) or the other accepts all your needs immediately and spontaneously (which is very unlikely).

A phenomenon with extremely complex, indeterminate, unpredictable, and changing characteristics, such as any human activity created equally from concrete factors (needs, goods, and interests) and abstract factors (sensations, emotions, and perceptions), negotiation therefore seems difficult to describe in a clear, coherent, and exhaustive notion. It is much easier to identify its etymological origin, which in Italian is the same as that of shop ("*negozio*"): both coming from Latin "*nec otium*" = non-idleness, i.e. work (whereas in ancient Rome the term "*otium*" did not have the same meaning that the word "idleness" has today, but referred to any kind of pleasant activity, artistic, cultural or spiritual, other than trade and business).

Beyond the common meaning of the term, almost every author or scholar on negotiation has attempted their own interpretation. Hence the very wide variety of definitions (almost all reflecting, however, only partial angles of the phenomenon), which can be summarized broadly in three types of notions:

a) those which highlight negotiation's psycho-sociological contents of interrelationship and communication;

b) those which prefer to emphasize its decision-making aspect;

c) those which give priority to its nature as a conflict management tool.

On the other hand, inspired by its constituent elements and at the same time all its aspects (in the absence of only one of which, as we will see below, there is no negotiation, but other and different cases), our definition of "*negotiation*" is as follows:

"*A process of activity of two or more parties, holders of divergent but interdependent interests concerning a common issue, aimed at reaching an agreement on the same issue through reciprocal concessions*"[14].

Let us see it now broken down and analysed in its different components.

a) *A process of activity*: it is the "nature" of negotiation, which consists of a whole series of activities carried out by the parties in a consequential order aimed at the final agreement, some of which have immediate legal value (e.g. an irrevocable concession or partial agreement on one point of negotiation) and others are legally irrelevant (e.g. an emotional reaction or a non-binding proposal or other mere declarations). The meta-legal nature of this definition also evokes the division of negotiation into different phases of time and helps to clarify the substantial difference between the term "negotiation", which is the whole process, and the term, often mistakenly used as a synonym, of "bargaining", which represents only one of the central and decisive phases of the negotiation itself.

---

[14] Giovanni Polizzi, *La funzione del negoziatore: profilo e problemi giuridici (The negotiator's function: profile and legal problems)*, in Review *Il Nuovo Diritto* no.10/95, Abilgraf, Rome, October 1995.

b) *of two or more parties, holders of:* they are the negotiating "subjects", which are referred to as "parties" (as in contractual terminology), almost never being individuals, but delegations made up of several persons, and even of subjects who do not participate directly at the negotiating table (such as those responsible for the final approval of the agreed text or the natural or legal persons for whom the negotiation has been undertaken), provided that they are "holders" of the same interests that underlie the negotiation.

The *parties* can then be defined as "centres of analogous interests": similar, not identical, because the individual subjects who make up a negotiating party certainly have a common interest in the successful conclusion of the negotiation, but often each of them for different reasons aimed at satisfying their own interests.

Depending on the number of parties, the negotiation may be "*bilateral*" (if there are two parties) or "*multilateral*" (if there are more than two). The latter, as we will see below, although with internal phases, procedures and dynamics partly similar to those of bilateral negotiation, nevertheless takes place in a different organizational context, with a different operational purpose and with different strategies.

c) *divergent but interdependent interests:* these are the "grounds" for negotiation which, in defining interest as "the inner motivation to seek satisfaction of a need through the acquisition of the goods considered most suitable", move individuals or groups or nations to pursue the acquisition of such goods precisely through negotiation. In this respect, it is commonly stated that interests are not only the grounds, but also the "units of measurement" of each negotiation.

In fact, in a technical sense, there are two types of interest in each negotiation:

1) the "*interest in negotiating*", understood as "the reason that makes a negotiated solution to the issue more useful than, or just as useful as (if you invest in the relationship), any other non-negotiated, unilateral or bilateral, alternative solution";

2) and the "*negotiating interests*", understood as "the modalities of a possible understanding perceived and pursued as optimal".

The first type of interest, which is based on the problem of alternatives, is the real driving force behind the whole negotiation process. According to Fisher, Ury, Patton, and their Harvard school followers, the concept of alternative is fundamental in any negotiation. It goes back to their famous *Getting To Yes: Negotiating Agreement Without Giving In* (1981), of which we will say more later, the conception, for the first time in the theory of negotiation studies, of a BATNA (*Best Alternative To a Negotiated Agreement*) - in Italian language AMAN (*Alternativa Migliore a un Accordo Negoziato*) or for others MAAN (*Migliore Alternativa a un Accordo Negoziato*) - as a measure of whether or not it is convenient to negotiate and, once negotiation has begun, as a constant benchmark for whether or not it is convenient to conclude it. The strengthening or weakening of BATNA at the various stages of negotiation would also be closely linked to the strengthening or weakening of "negotiating power" towards the counterparty. So:

- if the interest in negotiating is greater than BATNA, you must negotiate;
- if the two elements have the same degree of importance, you can negotiate, or you must if you want to strengthen the interpersonal relationship with your counterparty;
- if the interest in negotiating is less than BATNA, there is no longer any convenience in negotiating.

It is always good practice to evaluate one's own BATNA in advance and, if it is known or it can be known, that of the counterparty, and always pay great attention to any changes in these alternatives throughout the negotiation (for example: suppose you acquire, during a sale negotiation, another potential customer who has already communicated their terms to you: these will be your BATNA in the ongoing negotiation with the first customer). However, some authors[15] have put the concept of BATNA under a thorough critical analysis, deeming it outdated or, if applied uncritically and too simplistically, much less useful than it seems.

Again, in our definition of negotiation, interests are described as "divergent but interdependent":

"*divergent*" (not different, otherwise there could not be a negotiation) as they are "perceived as having the same object but a conflicting configuration";

"*interdependent*" as "their realization necessarily requires the counterparty's (active or passive) contribution".

The measure of the divergence defines the "area of possible understanding" (called ZOPA = *Zone Of Possible Agreement*); while the qualification of interests reflects the same duality of the negotiation: divergence as a factor of "competition", interdependence as a factor of "cooperation".

Finally, it should be noted that, if interests were not divergent but similar, there would be no negotiation but "consultation"; whereas, if they were divergent but not interdependent, there would be "conflict".

d) *concerning a common issue*: it is the "object" of negotiation on which the parties seek an agreement. If the term "issue" highlights the breadth of the object, the adjective "common" underlines the

---

15 In particular: Jim Camp, *Start With No: The Negotiating Tools That the Pros Don't Want You to Know*, Crown Business, New York, 2002.

fact that the subject of each negotiation is in itself a problem to be solved, possibly jointly, regardless of the quality of the relationship existing between the parties.

The extreme variety in the use of negotiation as an instrument for decision-making, conflict-resolution, and enhancement of a common commitment to cooperation makes it possible to categorise the negotiations precisely according to the nature of the issue that their regard. There are therefore political negotiations (between institutional actors of the State or between political parties or other similar forces), political-diplomatic (international intergovernmental negotiations), economic or more specifically commercial (often erroneously defined only as bargaining), social (between the State and the social partners, employers' representatives and trade unions or trade associations, etc.), cultural (for the management of resources or for the planning of major artistic and cultural events), organizational (which take place within a company for the distribution of responsibilities and resources, or for operational planning objectives), and so on.

Anything that is equally important and necessary for two or more parties can become the object of a negotiation.

It sounds like a tautology, but even negotiation itself can sometimes be the object of negotiation. This is the case of the so-called "*talks about talks*", a not uncommon but recurring case in the political-diplomatic landscape, usually after a long and hard conflict, whenever two or more political actors, including international actors, have to decide whether or not to open a real negotiation of peace and substance, when and where to open it, under what conditions and in what forms.

e) *aimed at reaching an agreement on the same issue*: it is the negotiating "goal", meaning by "agreement" an "agreed solution to the issue under negotiation". Unlike the term "agreement" indicating the specific instrument (Treaty, Agreement, Protocol, Memorandum of Understanding, Exchange of Notes, Minutes, Contract, etc.) in which the "understanding" is substantiated, the latter term is more general and all-encompassing, since it covers all types of consent, expressed verbally or in writing in any type of document.[16]

Once reached, the final agreement satisfies the interest in negotiating of both negotiating subjects, but it should be understood that it never fully satisfies their negotiating interests, some of which have been sacrificed, precisely in order to reach agreement, on the altar of reciprocal concessions.

It should also be noted that, if there were no search for an agreement, there would be no negotiation but "discussion" (an absolute statement of one's own positions, as is often the case in private relations); whereas, if the understanding were replaced by a consensus imposed by force, it would be a "diktat" (as is often the case on the international stage).

An agreement may be comprehensive or partial (if it resolves the whole problematic issue or only part of it), substantive or procedural (if it resolves questions of substance or only of procedure, such as the place and timing of the negotiation, agenda, etc.), final or temporary (if destined to enter into force definitively once formalized or if subject to an initial or final term), absolute or conditional (if free from modal elements or subject to suspensive or resolutive conditions: strictly speaking, almost all international agreements are "conditional" undestandings, since they are intended to enter into force only as a result of the respective ratification by the parties), binding or non-binding, and so on.

Two particular types of non-binding agreement, recurrent in the panorama of both internal (especially political or trade union-related) and international negotiations, are the so-called "*understanding ad referendum*" and the rather rare "*agreement to disagree*".

The first is used when the text of an understanding agreed between the negotiators still has issues to be resolved, the decision

[16] For practical reasons we will make use hereafter of both terms, agreement and understanding, as synonyms.

of which is up to the respective central authorities. The character of an "understanding *ad referendum*" can refer to:

a) the whole text, which in this case must contain a specific article providing for the suspensive condition resulting from the need to "report" the draft agreement to the higher authority for consultation and/or decision;

b) or one or more points in the text itself, which must in that case appear in the draft agreement drawn up in square brackets.

Quite different is the case of the so-called "agreement to disagree". This is a rather unusual act, almost always drawn up not in the form of agreement but of minutes of what was recorded during the negotiation. It can be used by the parties, if it is impossible to reach agreement, at least in order to highlight by consensus the reasons for or points of disagreement, to safeguard the quality of the relationship and the level of communication between them, to provide a useful instrument for a possible and subsequent round of negotiations and, last but not least, to enable the negotiators to report back to their principals at least a minimum concrete result, "saving face" in front of the media and public opinion.

Any kind of final agreement, in order to become binding on the parties, must at least go through two other stages: formalization and ratification. The "*formalization*" of the agreement consists of the "*subscription*" (i.e."signature") by those who are provided with the so-called "full powers", possibly *preceded by the "initialing*" by the negotiators themselves (to take stock definitively of its text by authenticating it). The "*ratification*" may take forms of minor or greater officiality depending on who is called upon to carry it out (negotiator's hierarchical superior, superordinate body or institution or, in the case of international treaties, the Head of State, "when necessary, subject to the authorization received from the Parliament", in Italy under articles 80 and 87 of the Constitution) or may not even be necessary, in those numerous cases where the entry into force of the document has been explicitly linked only to its signing.

f) *through reciprocal concessions*: they are the "instruments" of negotiation, through which agreement is reached. Concessions which the parties seek, offer, request, negotiate and exchange during the course of the negotiation, and which must be understood as "deliberate changes of position ("formal" concessions) or deliberate weakening/suppression of a negotiating interest ("substantial" concessions), to the advantage of counterparty's requests and in view of the achievement of a compromise (on a point of negotiation), or of the final agreement".

It must be borne in mind that, as is the case with the repeated administration of a good to satisfy a need, so in the negotiation, concessions normally have a decreasing utility. Indeed, while the former are of fundamental importance to strengthen the interpersonal relationship between the negotiators and begin to channel the negotiation in a positive direction, with their increase in quantity or value they gradually distance the negotiators from their respective "maximum sustainable positions" (MSP) bringing them closer to their respective "minimum acceptable results" (MAR) and risking reaching a point where such MARs could be inferior to their BATNA and eliminate or almost eliminate the utility of the negotiation itself.

Finally, with regard to the concept of "*reciprocity*", it cannot be understood in the sense of equivalent importance, since in a negotiation the value of a concession is always perceived subjectively, that is, to varying degrees, both by the person making it and by the recipient. In our opinion, concessions can be considered "mutual" only if "linked together by a temporal consequentiality and a balanced substantial connection": that is, characterized by a clear or implicit relationship of temporal causality and an equivalence of substance resulting from the balance between the values perceived by both parties. For example, two concessions, one (concrete and current) consisting of the approval of a proposal and the other (generic and future) of the commitment to "study" a counterparty's similar proposal could not be considered mutual.

It goes without saying that, if the concessions were only unilateral (of course by the weaker party), we would return to the aforementioned case of "diktat"; whereas, if an agreement were to be reached but without the need for concessions, we would be faced with an activity of "*problem solving*" (widespread in organizations, but in the business sciences often mistakenly confused with negotiation).

We believe that it is useful and important to recognize these and other interaction models and to identify each time their differences from genuine negotiation, both in order to practise recognizing truly negotiating or negotiable situations, and to be able to better understand and manage interactive cases other than that of negotiation without unnecessary or excessive expenditure of resources.

1.4. The negotiation profile in the Italian legal system, and its "reference praxis"

Inspired by respect for the principle of contractual autonomy, the Italian legal system does not provide for specific negotiating rules, except for:

a) the negotiator's legal issues;

b) two basic principles to be followed by any negotiation, "*good faith*" and "*fault-less reliance*" (the violation of which results in a pre-contractual liability or, as the Romans said, *culpa in contrahendo*, as well as the obligation to pay the fault-less counterparty damages);

c) certain cases governed by law, consisting of activities with similar characteristics but not equal to those of negotiation.

The negotiator's legal issues will be raised in the next chapter.

As for the principles to which any correct negotiation must respond, these can be directly deduced from the discipline of the "Contracts in general" (art.1321 and seq.), referred to in Title II of Book IV ("Obligations") of the current Civil Code[17]: in particular from what is provided by articles 1337 ("Negotiations and pre-contractual liability") and 1338 ("Knowledge of causes of invalidity"), which it seems useful to quote in full.

Art. 1337 provides that "In the conduct of negotiations and forming the contract, the parties shall behave in good faith."

Then, art. 1338 reads: "The party who, knowing or who should know the existence of a cause of invalidity of the contract, has not informed the other party shall pay it damages suffered for having relied, without fault of their own, on the validity of the contract."

It is interesting to note that the reference of the Civil Code to the concept of "good faith" and to the principle of "fault-less reliance" in the private discipline of contracts evokes a similar reference to that "good faith" taken into great consideration by international law in conducting negotiations and concluding

---

[17] In the text in force as of May 2008.

agreements between States. We will come back to these concepts later, in particular in the paragraph devoted to the so-called "diplomatic method".

With regard to other cases which result in activities similar to those of negotiation, and while reserving further discussion of para-negotiating activities of the third party, the civil law category of the so-called "*contracts aimed at settling a dispute*": and that is, the "transaction" referred to in articles 1965-1976; and the "transfer of assets to creditors", provided for by articles 1977-1986.

While the latter, aimed at avoiding enforcement proceedings, consists of a "contract by which the debtor instructs their creditors or some of them to wind up all or some of the former's assets and to distribute among themselves the proceeds in satisfaction of their claims" (art. 1977), much more interesting seems to us the notion of "*transaction*", aimed at avoiding a judgment following a cognizance action and described by art. 1965 as follows:

"1. The transaction is the contract by which the parties, by making mutual concessions, put an end to a dispute that has already begun or prevent a dispute that may arise between them. 2. Mutual concessions may also create, modify or extinguish relationships other than that which has been the subject of the parties' claim and dispute."

Transaction therefore that, like negotiation, works through mutual concessions and is even likely to create new options and expand the area of negotiation itself and understanding.

A final mention should be dedicated here, by way of related argument, to the recent publication, on June 7, 2019, of the "Reference Praxis" UNI/PdR 59:2019 entitled "Negotiation activities – Negotiation process, negotiator's requirements and operational guidelines for conformity assessment"[18]. Although it is not a real prescriptive document, it is still useful to look at it.

The text defines the concept of negotiation and its distinctive features with respect to other methods of managing opposing interests, and the negotiation process; specifies the role and requirements of the negotiator in terms of knowledge, skills and competences; it provides, lastly, training guidelines as well as operational guidelines for assessing the negotiator's compliance with the defined requirements.[19]

---

[18] The so-called "reference praxis" are among the "products of European standardization", as provided for by EU Regulation no.1025/2012, and are national para-regulatory documents that introduce technical requirements or sectoral application models of technical standards, elaborated under the operational management of the UNI (Italian National Unification Agency) and issued by it.

[19] Press release of 7 June 2019 from the website www.uni.com.

1.5. The negotiator's profile, particularly in the Italian legal system

The first important aspect of the negotiator's legal profile is the very nature of the activity carried out by the subject: activity – as we have already said - of a meta-legal nature, but not legally irrelevant. On the contrary, it is activity which produces liability and potentially legal effects regardless of any possible outcome of the negotiation (think of the aforementioned *culpa in contrahendo*) and that, for this reason, the legal system subjects to verification and control. Apart from the case of those who negotiate directly in their own interest, it is therefore legitimate to adapt the concept of "function", as an activity to which law attaches legal importance on the whole requiring control.

The negotiator is in charge of a twofold order of relations: with the counterparty and with the sending subject (or the organization to which they belong).

On the one hand, they are the bearer of mere "expectations" (obviously not protectable by law) about a successful outcome of the negotiation, but they are also the holder of a real "legitimate interest" (protectable and protected) regarding the observance of the principle of good faith and that unwritten code of ethics to which any correct negotiation must be inspired.

To the organization to which they belong (or private sending subject), the negotiator is bound by a pre-existing internal relationship, called "management relationship". Whether it is an organic relationship with the body to which they belong (as in the case of diplomatic agents and other officials of the Public Administration or operators of commercial companies), whether it is an employment contract or a company relationship or a mandate contract with representation or even a simple informal assignment, an internal relationship always pre-exists the sending of the negotiator and is the source of their particular power of representation.

As a "representative", the negotiator holds a power of substitution in other legal activity comparable to that provided for by "direct representation", in which - as is well-known - the effects of the act occur directly in the sphere of the represented party. In fact, outside the case of those who negotiate on their own behalf, the negotiator always deals "on behalf and in the name" of the sending subject (it is unthinkable that rights and obligations arising from an international treaty or a trade agreement could be attributed personally to the actors of the negotiation!). Moreover, even in the case of the negotiator, as in that of the representative, the law or customary practice provide for various procedures for the attribution and proof of the representative power (so-called "accreditation", whose effects are similar to those of the "power of attorney"), as well as different methods of "verification of credentials".

However, the negotiator is not a normal representative, since in direct representation the power of replacement is attributed in view of the conclusion of a given act, i.e. under an obligation to act. But the negotiator, if they deem it appropriate, may also withdraw from the negotiating table with no outcome, or accept a simple "agreement to disagree", or conclude a partial agreement different or more limited than that which was the prescribed objective of their assignment.

Then, it is necessary to refer to other possible institutions, the most appropriate of which seems to be that of "authorization": not that provided for by administrative law, but that particular "legal act under private law, with which a person confers on another the power to carry out legal acts aimed at influencing the sphere of the authorizing person, but in the name of the authorized person. The latter, therefore, is empowered, not compelled to act, and this attribute makes them different from a representative."[20]

---

[20] Andrea Torrente, *Manuale di Diritto Privato (Manual of Private Law)*, Giuffrè, Milan, 1968.

Hence a new notion, unknown to the law and (like the notion of negotiation) with a meta-legal character: that of a specific "*negotiating representation*" power, which combines the widest power of replacement (as in direct representation) and the widest discretionary power (as in authorization).

Like any other natural person, also the negotiator, in order to carry out the required activity (function), must be provided with legal capacity (= suitability to be subject to rights and obligations), natural capacity (= mental capacity, i.e. full possession of their faculties) and capacity to act (= suitability to acquire and exercise, through their will, subjective rights and to assume obligations).

Thus considered in its entirety, the legal profile of the negotiator can therefore be summed up in the new expression, also so far unusual in the field of law, of "*negotiating capacity", i.e. legitimation to a given negotiation*, understood as the sum of legal capacity, natural capacity, capacity to act and negotiating representation power.

A form of additional capacity compared to the mere negotiating capacity is finally the *capacity, i.e. legitimation, to the formalization of the agreement*, which allows those who are provided with it (the negotiator themselves or another subject superordinate to them) to formalize the agreement by "initialling" it or, in the presence of "*full powers*", through its "signature" (at international level, there is no need for full powers only for heads of state, heads of government and foreign ministers, the latter competent for granting such powers to all other subjects).

Very frequent in negotiation reports is the use of the term "*negotiating mandate*", a legally improper expression, which has nothing to do with a genuine mandate relationship, but which is used to indicate "all instructions previously given to the negotiator regarding the purpose, content, and limits of their assignment".

Another completely extra-legal term, with which the new notion of negotiating capacity is unconnected, is the much debated "*negotiating power*", used to qualify "the ability to modify the counterparty's perceptions towards reaching an understanding as close as possible to one's own interests".

With regard to the problems of the negotiator's will, to this function too it seems possible to extend without excessive difficulty the regulatory framework provided for in the case of direct representation. Looking then at the principles of the traditional "theory of reliance", each understanding will be null and void in case of lack of will (negotiation for figurative or educational purposes, by way of a joke, or negotiation conducted under physical violence) which is clearly recognizable by the counterparty, valid in case of unrecognizable lack of will or divergence (mental reserve), cancellable (*ex nunc*) in case of defect of will (by essential and recognizable error, by *"dolus malus"* (bad faith) or by mental violence), and rescindable (*ex tunc*) in the event of expressions of will determined by a state of need or danger.

A case that is certainly interesting and theoretically conceivable, but in fact very unlikely, is that of a negotiation conducted by those who have not been previously legitimized to negotiate: that is, the figure of a "*falsus (fake) negotiator*", with a profile identical to that of the "*falsus procurator*" well known to legal doctrine. The understanding that may be reached will be in this case considered ineffective, unless ratified by the subject or organization of which the *falsus negotiator* has presented themselves as a representative. It does not, however, seem possible to extend to the function of the negotiator (and quite rightly so, just to think, for example, of the far-fetched and catastrophic consequences that would result in international diplomatic negotiations!) the principle which, in the event of non-ratification, nevertheless makes the *falsus procurator* responsible for compensation for damages in favour of the fault-less third party (art. 1398 Civ. Code), since the rules of conduct of any serious negotiation always require the opposite party to previously verify the whole negotiating capacity of their interlocutor by means that, in the well-known and consolidated practice of the negotiations, go far beyond the normal diligence of the "*bonus pater familias*".

Finally, it remains to consider the cases - not at all theoretical - of the "*misuse of power*" by the negotiator (in the event of exceeding the limits of the negotiating mandate) or of their possible "*conflict of interest*" with the sending organization (to favour another subject outside the negotiation or to favour themselves, as is possible in cases comparable to the well-known case of the so-called "*procurator in rem suam*"). The most appropriate solution would be, to all appearances, to adapt the private rules laid down for the representation act to those cases as well and, therefore, to consider the agreement reached by the negotiator with misuse of power ineffective unless ratified and any agreement reached in a conflict of interest situation with the sending entity cancellable at the latter's request.

But the problems are, in fact, much more complex, since the principle of "fault-less reliance" of the counterparty in the event of the negotiator exceeding the limits of the mandate and the recognizability of the conflict of interests, which are required by articles 1398 and 1394 Civ. Code, are criteria completely unrelated to the concrete practice of negotiation, where no one but the negotiator themselves and the sending entity can normally know the exact content and the real limits of the other's negotiating mandate.[21]

---

[21] Giovanni Polizzi, *La rilevanza dell'errore e dell'eccesso di potere nel negoziato (The importance of error and misuse of power in negotiation)*, in Review *Il Nuovo Diritto* no.12/95, Abilgraf, Rome, December 1995.

1.6. The para-negotiating activities of the third party, and the "mediation for conciliatory purposes"

Negotiating processes may sometimes be joined by a "third party" outside the negotiation which, at the request of the parties, carries out activities often incorrectly defined as "negotiating", since they have characteristics of interaction, communication and exploration of interests almost identical to those of negotiation, but which are not at all negotiation. And that is because the third party, by definition, is not, and cannot be, the holder of negotiable interests, nor can it make concessions or, finally, participate in the effects of the understanding reached by the parties (as a rule, as the Romans taught, *res inter alios acta tertio neque prodest neque nocet* = the act concluded between two parties does not benefit or harm the third party). These activities are certainly significant and sometimes of great importance, especially for the peaceful settlement of international disputes, but – it must be reiterated – they are not "negotiating" activities in the true sense of the word, and we will therefore define them as "para-negotiating".

There are four cases, of less or greater complexity and with less or greater power of interposition, but all with a common requirement: the "compromise consent" of the parties involved, i.e. the common decision to request the intervention of the third party, reached within an ongoing or potential negotiating context. Let us consider them below in detail.

- "*Good Offices*": a less complex case with a lower degree of interposition, it is based on the attempt, completely devoid of binding character, of a third party "*super partes*" (= impartial) to induce the parties of a dispute or a conflict to enter into, or return to, contact and to agree to the opening of negotiations.

- "*Mediation*": a more recurrent case, common to both the public and private fields, and which, in common language, is more frequently confused with negotiation.

In the private field, it is a specific contract against payment (since it provides for the reimbursement of expenses or the payment of a commission to the mediator) regulated by articles 1754-1765 of the Italian Civil Code and the content of which can be drawn from the same notion of "mediator" (art.1754: "It is mediator who connects two or more parties for the conclusion of a deal, without being bound to any of them by relationships of collaboration, dependence or representation").

In international law, it is an interposition activity of the third party which is more complex and incisive than that of good offices, since the mediator (a State *super partes* or the supreme body of a State or an international organization), after having explored in depth and separately both the positions and interests of the parties, can, indeed has to, propose a draft written agreement (so-called "final text"), which the parties are then free to accept or not to accept, but not to modify. The mediator's intervention is often required when the parties, given the "political" impossibility of carrying out acts that would be seen as a giving in to the claims of the opposite party, need some sort of external "pressure" to be "forced to negotiate" (a well-known example is the Camp David Agreement of 1978 between Egypt and Israel, which required 13 days of negotiations and 23 subsequent drafts by the Mediator, the US President).

It should be repeated that mediation must in no way be confused with negotiation since, as the etymology of the term suggests, the third-party "mediator" is a "*medium*", and that is, *at the same time, instrument and point of equidistance.* As such, at the risk of losing their authority and credibility, and although using with the parties similar methods of analysis of situations, exploration of interests, and creation of possible options, the mediator is not and cannot ever be a real negotiator, since they are not in fact the holder of any interest, on which they can or must make any kind of concession.[22]

- "*(International) conciliation*": so described in order to distinguish it from the private conciliation introduced in Italy by recent provisions (see below), conciliation acquires a particular importance especially in international law where, in addition to the figure of the individual conciliator, this activity is performed much more often by a specific "*Conciliation committee*", asked by the parties to carry out an examination of the dispute and the drafting of a non-binding resolution proposal, generally contained in a report. This is a diplomatic instrument of considerable moral importance, which is used to avoid possible solutions involving the use of force, and very often a decisive step towards a subsequent mandatory solution by arbitration.

- "*Arbitration*": a more complex case with a greater degree of interposition, arbitration occurs both in international and in national law (articles 806-840 of the Italian Code of Civil Procedure). Unlike the first three forms of para-negotiating activities, which have supplementary value for a negotiation process they aim to promote or facilitate, arbitration has instead a constitutive value, as it creates a legal situation that resolves the dispute, replacing the parties' non-agreement with the decision, mandatory and binding, contained in the arbitration judgment (called "*arbitration award*").

Arbitration between States is based on the parties' common will, expressed in the so-called "arbitration compromise" (a specific act of "compromise" or an "arbitration clause" contained

---

[22] Giovanni Polizzi, *Negotiation & Mediation: brevi note a margine di un Convegno (Negotiation & Mediation: brief notes on the sidelines of a Conference)*, in Review *Il Nuovo Diritto* no.12/95, Abilgraf, Rome, December 1995.

in the main act), to resolve the dispute before an arbitrator or arbitration panel chosen by themselves (as a rule, each of the two parties chooses its own arbitrator and the two chosen choose a third one, who will be the actual arbitrator), whose judgment they undertake to abide by.

In the path mapped out by the European Union towards a common conception of extrajudicial justice (see Directive 2008/52/EC of the European Parliament and of the Council of 21 May 2008), Italy has also aligned its internal legislation with Law No. 69 of 18 June 2009 and Legislative Decree for implementation No. 28 of 4 March 2010, both regulating mediation aimed at reconciling civil and commercial disputes concerning alienable rights: so-called "*mediation for conciliatory purposes*". The new legislation has brought not only significant changes in dealing with disputes by creating a tool to reduce recourse to the courts, but also a profound innovation of the very institution of mediation and its function.

In fact, beyond the traditional legal configuration of mediation referred to in the aforementioned articles of the Italian Civil Code, today art. 1 of Legislative Decree No. 28/2010 describes "mediation" as "the activity, no matter how called, carried out by an impartial third party and aimed at assisting two or more subjects both in the search for a friendly agreement for the settlement of a dispute, and in the drafting of a proposal for its resolution". "Mediator", continues the rule, is "the natural person or persons who, individually or collectively, carry out mediation while remaining devoid, in any case, of the power to deliver judgments or decisions binding the recipients of the service". Finally, "conciliation" is "the settlement of a dispute following the conduct of mediation". In other words, while mediation remains an activity, conciliation is no longer, as in international law, another form of third party interposition, but becomes the desirable agreement resulting from the mediation itself.

Mediation for conciliatory purposes, which takes place in public or private bodies (including in mediation bodies set up by professional associations or chambers of commerce) registered in a special register held at the Ministry of Justice, can be of three types:

1) "optional", i.e. chosen by the parties;

2) "delegated", when it is the judge who invites the parties to attempt mediation;

3) "mandatory", when in order to proceed before the court, the parties must have previously tried it without success.

The law provides for this obligation in cases of disputes concerning: condominiums, real rights, division, inheritances, family agreements, lease, loan, company rent, compensation for damage resulting from the circulation of vehicles and boats, medical liability, and defamation by means of the press or other means of publication, insurance, banking and financial contracts.

The mediation procedure is introduced by an application to the body freely chosen by the parties and has a maximum duration of four months.

The agreement reached with the cooperation of the mediator is approved by the judge and becomes enforceable. In the event of non-agreement, the mediator can make a proposal for the resolution of the dispute which the parties remain free to accept or not.

1.7. Conflict: phenomenology, notion, and its constituent elements

It has already been said that negotiation, which arises almost always from a conflict situation, is the most effective means of peaceful resolution of the conflicts themselves. However, in order to learn how to manage and resolve a conflict peacefully, it is first necessary to recognize and analyse it. Our attention therefore now turns precisely to conflict: to this dimension of existence which, even when it is not violent or unarmed, is inherent in the reality of things and is also, like negotiation, an inescapable "category" of human action.[23]

"The human being - wrote Erich Fromm in 1973 - is the only animal that can kill or harm members of its species without any rational, biological or economic advantage"[24].

Indeed, on conflicts and wars, their causes, their developments and their outcomes, as well as the search for ways of preventing or resolving them, rivers of ink have always flowed, without these analyses having contributed in any way to reducing their impact in international or domestic reality. And, as always in the logic of contrasts, anyone who over the centuries has tried to theorize about the phenomenon of war could not help but turn their attention also to the phenomenon of peace, whose original concept, namely the absence of war (which today is defined as "*negative peace*"), has evolved since the early days to establish itself in more recent times as a complex of political-economic-social

---

[23] Giovanni Polizzi, *Guerra e Pace: un'alternativa chiamata "cultura del negoziato* (*War and Peace: an alternative called a "Culture of Negotiation"*, in Review *Nuova Voce del Rotary*, no.11, April 2018; as well as in *Proceedings of the Conference "Conflicts"*, organized by the Italian Geographical Society and the University "Niccolò Cusano"–telematics, Rome, 10-11 October 2018.

[24] Erich Fromm, *The Anatomy of Human Destructiveness*, New York, Holt, Rinehart and Winston, 1973; in Italian translation, *Anatomia della distruttività umana*, Mondadori, Milan, 1975-95.

conditions to ensure the order, well-being, and harmony amongst peoples (which can be summed up in the notion of "*positive peace*")[25].

As with the notion of negotiation, as well as in the vast literature on conflict, its definitions are perhaps as many as the authors themselves who have written about it. It is therefore appropriate, here too, to start from the etymological origin of the term, coming as always from Latin, and more precisely from the noun "*conflictus*", resulting from the past participle "*conflictum*" of the verb "*confligere*", that is, fighting. The etymology of the word already leads to two considerations. The first, of a lexical character, is that the very structure of the verb, composed of the preposition *cum* (with) and a rare verb *fligere* (to bump against), indicates that the conflict presupposes a relationship, that is, that conflict can only be talked about in the presence of at least two subjects (conflict with oneself, such as so-called negotiation with oneself, is not a conflict in the technical sense, but only a difficult aspect of a decision-making process between alternative choices). The second consideration, of a conceptual character, is that the term, in Italian as in Latin, is declined in the past (*conflictus* = "fought", and not fighting) and evokes therefore the causes of the contrast, and not its prospects of solution.

Having said that, the current definition that all dictionaries, at least those of the Italian language, give of the word "conflict", corresponding to its common sense, is that of "shock, contrast, opposition or struggle, most of the time left to fate in taking up arms"[26]; where, on the other hand, conflict necessarily means not only open violence, but also tension, disagreement, dissent or

---

25 The relationship between the two notions of peace has been particularly deepened by the Norwegian sociologist and mathematician Johan Galtung, especially in his fundamental *Storia dell'idea di pace* (*History of the Idea of Peace*), Pangea, Turin, 1995.

26 Devoto-Oli, *Dizionario della Lingua Italiana* (*Dictionary of the Italian Language*), Le Monnier, Florence, 1971-89.

divergence. Many scholars of negotiation understand as conflict exactly a divergence of interests and needs between two or more parties, which causes incompatible results for each of them. However, this definition does not take into account a fundamental element of conflict: subjective perception. In fact, Rubin's statement seems to us to be correct that, "since what matters is what people think about reality, beyond and more than reality itself, conflict must be defined not as a divergence of interests, but as the perception of a divergence of interests"[27].

This divergence of interests and needs, and the incompatibility of the results being pursued, may thus be based on objective reality (which the parties have examined, of which they are aware, but which they have not been able to resolve: "real conflicts") or subjective perceptions, sometimes fallacious or pre-designed (incorrect communications, incomplete information, misunderstandings, or even negative heritage from the past: "unreal conflicts"). As most researchers have correctly observed, when put to the test almost all conflicts contain elements that are both real and unreal. However, neither the perceived divergence of interests referred to in the above-mentioned definition nor many other definitions proposed by different authors are able to explain what gives rise to the divergence itself or its perception or the incompatibility of the results being pursued.

This is why we have considered it appropriate to adopt, while adding to it (in parentheses), the excellent definition given by the American sociologist Lewis Alfred Coser[28], according to which "*conflict*" is:

> "*A struggle over values or a claim of rights over scarce (or perceived as such) (tangible or intangible) resources (or almost always both elements together)*".

---

[27] Jeffrey Rubin, *Conflict from a Psychological Perspective*, in "*Negotiation Strategies for Mutual Gain*", Lavinia Hall, Harvard, 1993.

[28] L. A. Coser, *The Functions of Social Conflict*, 1956, cit.

Let us break down this notion and immediately look at what Coser describes in innovative terms a *struggle over values*. "Values" must be understood not only as national, political, religious, ethical or cultural values, but also all sorts of conceptions, beliefs, ideologies, consolidated visions, strong ideas and opinions, at both individual and collective level. This is undoubtedly the most demanding and dangerous category of conflicts, because it tends to be radical (values are such only for those who share them) and difficult to negotiate (every ideology, even the most tolerable and democratic, is by definition totalizing and always tends to replace, erasing it, any different or alternative ideology).

Let us move on to the *claim of rights*. The concept is multi-purpose and can adapt to any case - property, possession, use or other enjoyment – to which, always at both individual and collective level, one could or believe to be able to lay claim.

Rights over *resources*: a term which is deliberately generic but, as in the economic concept of "good", intended to indicate any means suitable for satisfying the need, whether individual or collective, and which, as we have said, may consist of something *tangible* (territory, house, sum of money, etc.) *or intangible* (professional position, consent, recognition, etc.).

The qualification of *scarce* then defines the economic character of the claimed resources, while the clarification (added by the writer) *or perceived as such* must be understood in the dual meaning of the perception of the object of the claim both in terms of scarcity and in terms of the resource itself, that is, of means actually suitable for satisfying that need.

It has been observed that there is hardly a conflict for resources perceived as abundant, "unless there are perceptions of serious iniquity and injustice in the distribution of resources, or the abundant resource being contested is but a pretext to compete for an implicit resource perceived as scarce"[29].

Or finally, as mentioned in our definition, the conflict can contain *almost always both elements together.*

As is objectively evident, the typology of conflicts is not only extremely varied, but also variable during the course of the conflict itself. Equally varied and variable are its contents, as numerous as the same needs and interests in order to satisfy which we face the conflict. Instead of its typology, it therefore seems more useful to focus the observation on the general and constant characteristics of the conflict phenomenon, which can be summarized as follows:

1) the conflict - as we have already said - is inherent in the reality of things and in human nature and is therefore inevitable at all levels, being able to involve two or more people, social groups, communities, populations or nation states;

2) each conflict always consists of two elements: a problem (most often a perceived divergence of interests caused by incompatible preferences regarding the distribution of a scarce resource) and a feeling of discomfort/resentment (caused by the problem or previous unresolved differences);

3) some authors add a third element, consisting of the existence of a situation of ambiguity: "in the rule" or "in the relationship" when there are, respectively, no clear and shared rules on how to resolve the conflict or a clear and shared hierarchy of roles that recognizes the legitimacy of one of the parties to arrange how to resolve the conflict[30];

4) the conflict (a basic observation in the study of negotiation) is most often the unavoidable result of the impossibility or inability to communicate in order to resolve the contrast in collaborative and constructive terms;

---

[29] Rino Rumiati and Davide Pietroni, *La negoziazione (Negotiation)*, Raffaello Cortina Editore, Milan, 2001.

[30] Rumiati and Pietroni, *op. cit.*

5) there is never a single objective cause of conflict, even if it seems so or even if only one cause is the trigger;

6) the parties involved in the conflict do not always have a clear perception of the object of the struggle, since each instinctively relates the dispute to its own system of values and judgment: each, that is, automatically creates its own representation of the situation, the so-called "conflict scheme", deriving from its own personality, the quality of the relationship with the opposite party, the perception of the interests at stake and similar past experiences.

Since we are on the subject of the psychology of conflict, it seems to us useful to spend a few more comments on the different logical structures that a conflict can assume depending on its size and type. And, since every good negotiator must have at least a basic knowledge of the problems and decision-making mechanisms of their own side and of the counterparty, we will start with what - as we have said - is not a conflict in a technical sense.

These are the so-called "*intra-personal*" conflicts, which psychologists call "intra-psychics", if they concern conflicting desires or objectives of which the subject is aware, and which psychoanalysts instead define as "psychic" or "dynamic", if they occur at an unconscious level, and then emerge at the conscious level spontaneously or as a result of psychotherapy. Each intra-personal conflict presents the individual with a painful decision among four types of alternative choices:

1) "approach-approach": between two desired objects or goals of equal attractiveness, incompatible with each other, that is, both impossible to be achieved together (e.g. I want to buy a new car, but I am undecided between two models both of which I like);

2) "removal-removal": between two rejected objects or goals of equal adverse force, incompatible with each other, that is, both impossible to be refused together (e.g. I do not want to spend money to repair the old car, but I do not want accidents to happen to me);

3) "approach-removal": between two desired and rejected objects or goals incompatible with each other (e.g. I want a new car, but I do not want to spend money) or between two aspects, one attractive and the other adverse, of the same object or goal (e.g. I want that sports car, but I do not want it to be so uncomfortable);

4) "double approach-removal": between two incompatible objects or goals, each of which has both attractive and adverse aspects (e.g. I want to buy a new car, but I am undecided between two cars, each with equivalent merits and defects): a case that happens very frequently in everyday life.

Different from intra-personal conflicts are "*inter-personal*" ones, which occur between two or more people if the satisfaction of a desire or the achievement of a goal by the individual comes into conflict with the desires or goals of other subjects. Inter-personal conflicts are therefore all those that go beyond the inner dimension and whose typology is, in general, the subject of study by other disciplines (anthropology, sociology, social and labour psychology, political and economic sciences or, as regards the relationship between States, the science of international relations). These are the real conflicts in the technical sense, which to a greater and greater extent can also acquire the nature of armed conflicts.

For their proper evaluation it is always useful to bear in mind the concept of claiming rights over scarce resources and to consider that, beyond its size and complexity, every conflict, in an extremely simplified form, generally turns out to be a struggle for:

1) the acquisition of goods or the realization of goals which are identical for both sides (e.g. both Tom and Dick want X);

2) or for the acquisition of goods or the realization of goals, both different but incompatible (e.g.: Tom wants X and Dick wants Y, which in turn can be:

2a) in a positive sense, something different from but incompatible with X;

2b) or, in a negative sense, the simple non-acquisition of X by Tom)[31].

Again in a simplified form, it is useful to observe how, also from the point of view of human reactions to a conflict situation, the basic mechanisms are more or less the same, regardless of the size or level of the conflict (from interpersonal to international). Among the different theories, two deserve to be taken into more careful consideration.

The first theory, called the "Horney triangle" (named after German psychoanalyst Karen Horney, who formulated it in 1945[32]), states that, in the face of any conflict situation, there would be no alternative to one of the three options she summarised in her "primary impulse triangle":

1) "go away" (flight),
2) "go towards" (submission), or
3) "go against" (fight).

The instinctive impulse of each individual facing a conflict would therefore be, depending on their strength or self-interest, only to avoid, suffer or contend with it. And beyond the first hypothesis, obviously unsuitable for resolving the conflict, there would be no other option but those of surrender, more or less conditional, or struggle, always long, expensive and devastating. The Horney triangle is a theory of fundamental importance in behavioural analysis and above all in the concrete definition of our

[31] Giovanni Polizzi, *Dal conflitto al negoziato* (*From conflict to negotiation*), in Review *Affari Esteri*, no.110, Janusa Editrice, Rome, April 1996.

[32] Karen Horney, *Our Inner Conflicts: A Constructive Theory of Neurosis*, Norton, New York, 1945.

concept of the "culture of negotiation", which in fact makes it possible to escape the nefarious triangle.

The second, called "Christiansen's dual theory" (named after the Norwegian psychologist and university lecturer Bjorn Christiansen, who formulated it in 1959[33]), results in a double assessment of the basic psychological reactions to conflict, in terms of attribution of responsibility and of expectations of solution. From the first point of view, the human beings would instinctively attribute responsibility for a conflict situation, alternatively and in priority order:

1) to others, or
2) to themselves, or
3) to others, whom they are nevertheless willing to understand.

With regard to the expectations of a solution, they would also be alternatively three:

1) waiting for the conflict situation to be resolved by others, or
2) taking initiative to resolve it, or
3) waiting for the situation to resolve itself.

Christiansen's dual theory is also of considerable importance and usefulness in the study of negotiation, especially to acquire awareness of one's own characteristics and tendencies at the negotiating table.

---

[33] Bjorn Christiansen, *Attitudes towards Foreign Affairs as a Function of Personality*, University Press, Oslo, 1959.

1.8. Conflict as an opportunity for growth and a factor for development

Conflict is almost always interpreted as a negative phenomenon, synonymous with discomfort, struggle, if not violence. It will therefore seem somewhat paradoxical to say that, nevertheless, conflict can also be a powerful factor of creativity and development and that, according to a positive approach quite widely shared among scholars - both in interpersonal and international relations there is now a great deal of talk about "*conflict transformation*" - it can represent a multidimensional phenomenon, a typical symptom of change and transformation within a society.

Many theorists of "conflict transformation"[34] believe that, when a conflict occurs, it changes or transforms those events, those subjects and those relationships that caused it to begin. The cause-and-effect link would be two-way: from the subjects and their interrelationships to the conflict and from this to the subjects and their interrelationships. Conflicts change relationships between subjects, transform their perceptions by accentuating their differences, distort communication methods and models of social organization, and modify images of the self and the other. Effective action can therefore be taken by enucleating these differences in a constructive way and aiming to deepen mutual knowledge, despite the persistence of disagreements and even irreconcilable needs, values and interests between the parties.

Without reaching the excessive optimism of those who say that conflict is even desirable because a conflictual relationship presupposes at least the existence of a relationship, the argument that the conflict can also be an opportunity for change and growth and that it helps to strengthen relations within the groups to which it belongs does not appear to be groundless. Indeed, there is now

---

[34] For all, John Paul Lederach, *Preparing for Peace: Conflict Transformation across Cultures*, Syracuse University Press, New York, 1995.

broad evidence that, especially within organizations, companies or offices, conflict is often a stimulus to innovation and increased efficiency and productivity.

Very significant in this respect is the result of a detailed survey carried out by the American scholar Richard Pascale, between 1982 and 1987, on 43 "excellent" American companies[35], from which it emerged that, over the five-year period under review, those which had experienced intelligently overcome internal conflict situations or events were the companies which had improved their competitiveness most of all, having been able to adapt promptly better than the others (some of which even failed) to changing market needs.

Conversely, and beyond Pascale's research, also from the analyses of other scholars[36] it has become clear that many and different can be the negative effects of forced suppression of conflict within organizations: inhibition of resourcefulness and innovation, contraction of individual and group creativity, deterioration in interpersonal relationships and intra-company communication, and a strong reduction in the quality of decision-making processes.

After all, conflict itself has neither necessarily negative nor positive effects: it is the way in which it is dealt with and managed that can make it an event of open clash and fracture, or a useful opportunity for comparison and a growth and development factor.

---

[35] Richard T. Pascale, *Managing on the Edge: How the Smartest Companies Use Conflict to Stay Ahead*, Simon & Schuster, New York, 1990.

[36] The Dutch C.K.W. De Dreu and M.K. De Vries, *Using Conflicts in Organizations*, University Press, Amsterdam, 1993.

Part Two

METHODOLOGY OF NEGOTIATION

2.1. Negotiation between competition and cooperation

In dealing with the nature of negotiation, we have already made reference to the tension arising from the coexistence in it of the two aspects of "competition" and "cooperation". Here it is worth explaining where these two opposing aspects originate from.

We negotiate - we have seen in Part One - whenever the satisfaction of a need or the realization of our interest require the (active or passive) involvement of another subject, in relation to a (tangible or intangible) asset also subject to (divergent but interdependent) interest of the counterparty and of which (subjectively or objectively) we perceive the scarcity.

In the absence of a better alternative to negotiation (BATNA), and having discarded the hypothesis of a flight from the conflict, a surrender or the use of force that we cannot afford (Horney), we resign ourselves to facing a negotiation that in our hearts we consider as made necessary by the "competition" with the counterparty to gain the contested resource.

However, it is precisely that condition of interdependence in which the achievement of our objectives is in relation to those of the counterparty that leads us to explore the possibility of gradual "cooperation", in order to identify how to divide the contested resource with the greatest possible satisfaction for both of us.

Principles and modalities for being able to face and manage any negotiating situation by facilitating its gradual evolution from competition to cooperation have been and continue to be the subject of different methodologies[37] inspired by different approaches. We will deal here below with three of them, the most

---

[37] According to its consolidated sense, we too mean, by the term "methodology", both the theoretical consideration of all the principles of method on which the discipline of negotiation is based, and the consequent ways of using those same principles and criteria within the framework of a well-defined operational method.

valuable and useful aspects and operational criteria of which will be summarized later on.

a) The Carnegie method for managing interpersonal relationships

As already mentioned, in 1936, in that particular cultural context known as "Human Relations Movement", an American teacher of *effective speaking and human relations*, named Dale Carnegie (1888-1955), published in 5,000 copies a book entitled "*How to Win Friends and Influence People*"[38]: a work which is not about negotiation, but which is still fundamental today for any scholar of negotiation or actual negotiator. In a few months Carnegie's text saw 17 reprints and became the "Bible of American Managers". From this to becoming an international best-seller the journey was short, to the point that by the death of its author in 1955 (the subsequent editions from 1964 onwards were revised and updated by his wife Dorothy) the book had already been translated into 31 languages, had sold 5 million copies and about half a million people had attended Carnegie's course. Today the text records over 15 million copies sold worldwide; the organization "*Dale Carnegie Training*" is a multinational company present in more than 90 countries[39] and an important global reference point in the field of management training courses. So great is the continuing interest aroused by the book that in 2012, on the occasion of the centenary of the establishment of the course, the "*Dale Carnegie & Associates*" considered it useful to revisit the contents of the original work and

[38] Dale Carnegie, *How to Win Friends and Influence People,* lastly Simon & Schuster, New York, 1981; since 1938 in Italian translation, *Come trattare gli altri e farseli amici,* lastly Bompiani, Milan, 1992.
[39] Among which, since 2002, also Italy (www.dalecarnegie.it).

adapt them to the changed context of interpersonal relationships determined by the web's new realities.[40]

What, in particular, had inspired Dale Carnegie - as reported by himself in the original foreword - had been the results of a psycho-sociological investigation, coordinated for two years by the University of Chicago, which had revealed how the topic of greatest interest to the adult population, after health, was the possibility of developing skills in the field of human relations, both in the family and at work, in business and in all other social relationships.

On the other hand, another research carried out in those same years under the auspices of the "*Carnegie Foundation for the Advancement of Teaching*" and confirmed by subsequent studies of the "*Carnegie Institute of Technology*", had pointed out that "even in such technical lines as engineering, about 15 percent of one's financial success is due to one's technical knowledge and about 85 percent is due to skill in human engineering – to personality and the ability to lead people" (that today we would call "leadership").

The reason for the enormous and continuing success of the work is undoubtedly due to the fact that Carnegie's book and method represent a very particular didactic system in 30 principles, made up of simple advice, sometimes apparently banal, but which in reality constitute an effective combination of applied psychology, techniques of interpersonal relationships and communication and persuasion strategies, easily applicable in any circumstance of life.

It therefore seems appropriate to describe at least the structure of the book, mentioning the principles that contain the most useful references to our reflection on negotiation.

---

[40] *How to Win Friends and Influence People in the Digital Age*, Dale Carnegie & Associates, Simon & Schuster, New York, 2011.

The work "How to Win Friends and Influence People" consists of four parts, preceded by "9 suggestions on how to get the most out of this book".

The first part illustrates the "3 Fundamental techniques in handling people": "Don't criticize, condemn, or complain (but try to understand why people do what they do)"; "Give honest and sincere appreciation"; "Arouse in the other person an eager want". All three principles are very useful in transforming competitive negotiating situations into cooperation.

The second part exposes the "6 Ways to make people like you", among which: "Become genuinely interested in other people" (fundamental to attempting the exploration of interests in a negotiation); "Be a good listener. Encourage others to talk about themselves" (a rule of behavior at the base of the technique of the so-called "active listening", that we will explain later on).

The third part presents the "12 Principles on How to win people to your way of thinking", including the following, which contain several suggestions useful to dampen aggressiveness in the bargaining: "Show respect for the other person's opinions. Never say, You're wrong!"; "If you are wrong, admit it quickly and emphatically"; "Get the other person saying "yes, yes" immediately" (a suggestion to always be borne in mind in the so-called "questioning technique", that we will explain later on too); "Let the other person feel that the idea is his or hers" (a tactic of great importance to gain the counterparty's final consent).

The fourth part finally describes the "9 Rules for being a leader: How to change people without giving offense or arousing resentment", among which: "Call attention to people's mistakes indirectly"; "Talk about your own mistakes before criticizing the other person"; "Ask questions instead of giving direct orders" (well-asked questions are the keystone of any bargaining); "Let the other person save face" (a rule of behaviour extremely important whenever we succeed in getting something significant from our counterparty).

b) The logical-mathematical method inspired by "game theory"

The method that more than others has characterized the studies on negotiation, still today authoritatively established and widespread, is the one that, focusing on the decision-making processes of the negotiators considered as "rational parties", makes use of the well-known "game theory": a branch of applied mathematics which studies the behaviour and decisions of (mainly economic) "rational" subjects in a context of "strategic interaction" (e.g. conflict, negotiation, etc.). Born of von Neumann's and Morgenstern's studies[41], analysed in depth by Nash especially with regard to "non-cooperative games"[42], and then further developed by Luce and Raiffa[43], "game theory" was applied for the first time to the study of negotiation by Bartos in 1974 in his "*Process and Outcome of Negotiations*"[44].

The coexistence in the negotiation of the two opposing aspects of competition and cooperation is at the root of the configuration of both "distributive" and "integrative" situations, which alternate and/or are repeated in every negotiating context. Let us remember that the two notions, although applied to the different type of negotiation rather than situation, were theorized for the first time in 1965 by the two sociologists Walton and McKersie[45] in a book, perhaps not by chance dedicated precisely to that category of negotiations, those involving trade unions, which are among the harshest and most difficult to conclude through an equal satisfaction of both social partners.

---

[41] John Von Neumann and Oskar Morgenstern, *Theory of Games and Economic Behavior,* Princeton University Press, 1944.

[42] John F. Nash, *Non-Cooperative Games*, University Press, Princeton, 1950.

[43] Robert D. Luce and Howard Raiffa, *op.cit.*

[44] Otomar J. Bartos, *op. cit.*

[45] R.E. Walton and R.B. McKersie, *A Behavioral Theory of Labor Negotiations*, McGraw-Hill, New York, 1965.

One defines as "*distributive*" those situations in which the parties, in strong competition, cannot (or do not know how to) do anything but to divide between themselves the resource under negotiation (like a pie of a fixed size) and as "*integrative*" those in which the parties, cooperating with each other, manage to expand the resource under negotiation (like a pie rising further) before dividing it.

The ambiguity of these situations can be represented, in a nutshell, with the well-known anecdote of the only orange left in the kitchen and of the two old sisters who fiercely argue over it, until the decision to split it in half. Then, separately, each of them hastens to peel their own half, but one throwing the peel and holding the pulp for an orange juice and the other throwing the pulp and holding the peel to sweeten a cake. That is a clear "distributive" situation, in which both parties have achieved an apparently satisfactory but in reality "sub-optimal" result, having wasted at the negotiating table (or rather in the rubbish bin!) 50% of the extra value that each could have obtained. If, on the other hand, the two sisters had managed to create an "integrative" situation by exploring their respective interests before the useless division of the orange, each of them would have obtained 100% of the desired value (of the pulp and peel), also raising together the value of the object by 200%.

If, by applying game theory, we consider two negotiators as two "rational parties", we can thus summarize the two different strategies adoptable as follows:

1) "claiming value" = "competition" = one negotiates to divide the resource trying to obtain more than the counterparty, i.e. to "maximize" one's own satisfaction = possible results: "win-lose" or "lose-win" (or even "lose-lose") = "zero-sum game" (in which one party's gain goes automatically to the detriment of that of the counterparty) = "distributive" situation or approach or type of negotiation: it is the characteristic of any dispute over a single scarce resource, namely any negotiating situation that appears to

have a single object; the two negotiators are "adversaries" and each pulls one end of the rope, moving from starting positions which are usually much more ambitious than the expected result; if the maximum position of one is higher than the minimum position of the other, there is a "zone of possible agreement" (ZOPA) and therefore room within which to negotiate; through subsequent mutual concessions, the agreement is likely to be halfway between the two original positions;

2) "creating value" = "cooperation" = one negotiates to increase the resource before dividing it, i.e. to "optimize" one's own and others' satisfaction = possible result: "win-win" = "variable sum game" (in which both parties increase, albeit in different proportions, their own gain) = "integrative" situation or approach or type of negotiation: it is the characteristic of any dispute in which the parties can generate alternative ideas of agreement and have recourse to various forms of compensation; the two negotiators are not adversaries, but "partners" working together to increase the object of the negotiating situation; if the options grow and differ, ZOPA becomes much wider and makes it possible to identify the most advantageous understanding possible for both parties.

As mentioned above, the difference between distributive and integrative negotiations can be based only on the diversity between the two objective situations underlying it or may be due to subjective factors specific to the negotiators, such as differences in character, personal style or approach to the problem. In theory, all negotiations which have, or appear to have, a single object (such as the price in a sale) objectively shape up to be distributive situations. In everyday life, however, it is much more frequent to have relationships and interactions which do not have a single object of negotiation or decision (such as contracts of various kinds, organizational restructuring, company mergers, international agreements, etc.) and therefore appear as potentially integrative negotiating situations, in which the parties can increase the objective value of the understanding before any division.

Moreover, as a seemingly distributive situation (precisely the case of the orange and the two sisters) could be integrative (if there had been "communication" between the two), so a potentially integrative situation can become distributive if the aspect of competition is left to prevail over that of cooperation.

Highly illustrative in this regard is the well-known "prisoner's dilemma" (two criminals accused of having committed a very serious crime, locked in two separate cells and offered by the police the choice to cooperate, confessing to the other's detriment), which the method applies to negotiation under the name of "*negotiator's dilemma*". Here we have two negotiators who, regardless of the characteristics of the situation in which they are engaged, must decide whether to adopt an integrative attitude of cooperation aimed at "creating value" or a distributive attitude of competition to "claim value" only to their own advantage. Well, although in theory "creating value" (which would give both a "good" result) is a more advantageous decision, it is more likely that each of the two decides to "claim" not knowing a priori the intentions of the other (for both in fact a "mediocre" result, which arises from two claims, is preferable to a "negative" one, which would be produced by cooperating with a competitive counterparty).

The difference between the two schemes is that, while in the prisoner's dilemma the two criminals find themselves in the material impossibility of communicating, in that of the negotiator the mediocre outcome of the negotiation stems from the lack of will or the inability to communicate of the two parties, who do not want or do not know how to explore their respective interests thoroughly.

And hence ultimately we see, beyond the canons of rationality which inspire the method: the frequent instinctive overvaluation of conflict; the "fear of losing everything, mirroring the counterparty's will to win hands down"[46]; attitudes of cautious reserve; simulations and tricks; and the widespread preference, even in the face of situations of potential collaboration, for a distributive approach and strategy, considered, however, to be much less risky[47].

c) Fisher and Ury's "principled negotiation" method

We have already referred to the distinguished role played in 1984 by Roger Fisher (1922-2012), as the most authoritative founding member of Harvard University's Research Center on Negotiation. But he also linked his name, in addition to many other important volumes on the subject, to the book written together with his student and then colleague William Ury (b. 1953) and published for the first time in 1981, entitled "*Getting To Yes: Negotiating Agreement Without Giving In*"[48]. The work, an international best-seller reprinted several times and, in recent editions, with the addition of Bruce Patton as the third co-author, is the greatest classic so far produced in terms of negotiation and, even today, an irreplaceable theoretical-practical guide behind most subsequent writings on negotiation. In fact, a very particular method is found there, well developed and widely exemplified, based on the concept of the so-called "*principled negotiation*" theorized by the authors.

It is certainly interesting to read the premises from which the insights of Fisher, Ury and Patton arose. "People find themselves in a dilemma. They see two ways to negotiate: soft or hard. The

---

46 Marco Mariani, *Negoziazione (Negotiation)*, Gruppo 24Ore, Milan, 2008.

47 Empirical research on a sample of 474 experimental negotiations conducted in Italy, reported by Mariani himself in the above-mentioned book, showed that 38% had been conducted in a distributive way, 35% mixed and 27% integrative.

48 R. Fisher and W. Ury, *Getting to Yes: Negotiating Agreement Without Giving In*, first published by Houghton Mifflin Company, USA, 1981 (then by Penguin Books, London and USA, in 1983; reprinted in 1991; and since 2011 together with B. Patton).

soft negotiator wants to avoid personal conflict and so makes concessions readily to reach agreement. He or she wants an amicable resolution; yet often ends up exploited and feeling bitter. The hard negotiator sees any situation as a contest of wills in which the side that takes the more extreme positions and holds out longer fares better. He or she wants to win; yet often ends up producing an equally hard response that exhausts the negotiator and his or her resources and harms the relationship with the other side." On the contrary, "there is a third way to negotiate – conclude the authors – a way neither hard nor soft, but rather both hard and soft: the principled negotiation method." Let us look at it in more detail.

We have already seen that a distributive negotiation determines a kind of "tug of war", the results of which can be placed at different points of an ideal "horizontal axis of confrontation" between the two extremes of "competition" and "cooperation". This is what almost always happens when negotiators fail to move away from their respective "positions" ("*positional bargaining*"), in which they even persevere and tend to lock themselves in, even going so far as to identify their own "ego" with the same and to become sensitive also to the need to "save face". Nor do intermediate positions seem to be of great help, with respect to the two extremes of the axis, for they always leave a sour taste in the mouth of both sides, being able to inspire balanced agreements, but almost always sub-optimal as only partially satisfactory (see the famous orange).

To the above two models, then, Fisher-Ury's method opposes a third one ("*interests bargaining*"), better able to create value and achieve a *win-win* result based on the potentially integrative nature of almost all negotiations. The model, defined as the "principled negotiation" or "negotiation on merits", can be summarized in the following four fundamental rules:

1) Separate the people from the problem (be soft with people, hard with the problem);

2) Focus on interests, not positions (explore interests);

3) Invent options for mutual gain (before deciding what to do);

4) Insist on using objective criteria (on which results must be based).

These are principles that still find themselves, more or less copied, paraphrased or reinterpreted, in many publications or writings dedicated to the study of negotiation. Forty years after the first publication of *Getting to Yes*, one may wonder what were, and still are, the reasons for their very extensive and continuing success. In our opinion, these three simple but basic findings by the authors themselves help us identify them: "Every negotiation is different, but the basic elements do not change. Principled negotiation is an all-purpose strategy. Unlike almost all other strategies, if the other side learns this one, it does not become more difficult to use; it becomes easier."

2.2. <u>Summary of assessment to identify our method</u>

From the analysis of the three methods of approach to negotiation issues described above, it was possible to draw several useful operational indications, all aimed at trying to transform as much as possible the competitive aspect of the negotiation activity into a cooperative one. However, one cannot help noticing how often such indications can sound somewhat incontrovertible and be guilty of excessive abstraction. It is therefore useful to attempt a summary of the three methodologies, trying to grasp the objectively most valid and usable contents, in order to identify for us a method that could be concise and effective in the face of any negotiating reality.

a) **Let us start with the first methodology**. Certainly a careful and constant application of Dale Carnegie's suggestions, to better deal with and manage interpersonal relationships, is an essential component of the psycho-cultural baggage of every good negotiator. In addition to making our communication as effective and persuasive as possible, the implementation of these teachings almost always ends up eliciting in our interlocutors, as if through a kind of strange mirroring effect, a better predisposition towards us and our arguments, making it less difficult to establish a climate of cooperation.

It is therefore strongly recommended to each negotiator to make use, in particular, of all those behaviours that help in:

- appreciating, but without excessive flattery, the ideas of your interlocutor;

- taking your time before replying, avoiding too abrupt or superficial reactions;

- encouraging the counterparty to talk about themselves and their expectations while listening carefully to their reasons (always remembering that, above all in negotiation, listening does not necessarily mean agreeing) and also making good use of the questioning technique;

- ultimately, motivating your counterparty to reach consensus making them appear as a co-creator of the understanding or vice versa, in the event of a not-so-positive outcome, helping them overcome the unwelcome situation and to save face.

b) **The second methodology, logical-mathematical**, presents us with the raw reality of negotiation: hard, difficult, often conflicting activity, continuous clash of minds, accompanied by a mix of sensations, emotions, perceptions and behaviours that shape and reshape it in alternating and recurrent phases, until some almost never obvious final outcome. It is certainly necessary to be able to recognize "distributive" situations and potentially "integrative" situations in order to manage them in the best possible way and to be able to take advantage of them, provided that we still have a clear idea of the abstract nature of certain schemes and models which, if applied to the end and with equal skill on both sides, end up leading to satisfactory but sub-optimal results: a bit like in chess matches (the number one logical-mathematical game) which, despite diagrams, patterns and rules, are never the same and that, if played by perfect automatons, end up with a "draw".

It should therefore not be ignored that in every negotiation process there are always both distributive and integrative situations and phases (the first most likely at the beginning, but also in the final phases of an integrative negotiation when it comes to distributing the realized added value); that model *win-win* of which for a few decades there has been a lot of talk is but a trend model, while *win-lose* or *lose-win* (if not even *lose lose*) situations are much more frequent; and that, ultimately, what makes the difference, even in negotiations, is always the unpredictability of the human factor.

The reality is that in fact negotiation is a form of activity always permeated by a dual ambiguity, because it has two dimensions, that we can describe oscillating and varying along two axes: one "horizontal" of competition-cooperation, which we have called the "*axis of confrontation*", and the other "vertical" of passivity-creativity, which we will call the "*axis of communication*".

And from the twofold dimension of negotiation let us change to the dual tension of the negotiator. Through the intersection of the two axes, the latter makes it possible to identify four so-called "basic styles of negotiation" which, defined by each author in its own way but with similar attributes, offer the schematic evidence of four different ways of relating to the aforementioned dual tension[49]:

the "Analytical" (competitive-passive),
the "Directive" (competitive-creative),
the "Accommodating" (cooperative-creative)
and the "Perfectionist" (cooperative-passive).

These are models, each with its own strengths and weaknesses: this is not the place to go into detailed descriptions, but it is nevertheless useful to outline at least their essential aspects for practical purposes.

The first feature, along the horizontal axis of the confrontation, is the difference in the respective priorities, that the Analytical and the Directive, both placed on the competition side, give to the goals to be achieved and that, on the contrary, the Accommodating and the Perfectionist, both more cooperative, attribute to the quality of interpersonal relationships. Hence also the inclination for working alone (typical of the more competitive Analytical and Directive) or to do teamwork (of the more cooperative Accommodating and Perfectionist).

---

49 Roberto Costantini and Raffaele Carso, *Negoziazione (Negotiation)*, Franco Angeli, Milan, 1993.

With regard to the vertical axis of communication, the Analytical, an excellent controller of their own emotions, lover of facts and rigorous programming (but often hesitant, detached, and unfit to react to changes) and the Perfectionist, idealistic, confident, and always looking for excellence (but often of narrow views, impractical and too self-critical, and dependent on others' judgments), both placed on the side of passivity, do not shine for mental openness to the unexpected, exploratory capability, and creative search for options. Different are the Directive, an innate leader, persevering, dynamic, and open-minded (but often too decision-maker, demanding and hypercritical, and attentive to a single solution) and the Accommodating, friendly, understanding, flexible, and simplifying (but often too prone to compromise, anxious, and unpredictable) who, being on the more creative side, are much more open to communication and exploration of each other's interests, as well as more easily inclined to seek options.

c) **Finally, as to the "principled negotiation" method by Fisher and Ury**, it should be borne in mind that lessons that can still be learned today from the classic *Getting to Yes* are so many and such as to consolidate its value as the main reference text in this field, especially with regard to the many suggestions that we also feel like agreeing to, although not entirely.

First of all, it is clear that, in the comparison between both types of negotiations on positions, soft or hard, and the type of negotiation on the merits, the latter, which is much more balanced than the former, is by far the preferable one to be adopted as a reference and to try to apply. In our method, therefore, we suggest assimilating its inspiring principles and practical contents, but provided that its character, even here, of a mere trend model is not overlooked, since the *win-win*, as we have already seen on several occasions, remains a result to which it is convenient to aim only to the extent that our interlocutor also shares this objective with us.

The two greatest insights of Fisher and Ury's method are, in our opinion, that of having clearly highlighted for the first time all the "subjectivity" of the negotiating phenomenon in its individual factors and complex personal implications, and that of having thoroughly explored its "objectivity" by removing the shell of the positions expressed and instead grasping the substance of the interests behind them.

Succeeding in separating the people from the problem (and above all keeping them separated throughout the course of the negotiation), and adopting a soft negotiating attitude towards the former and a hard one towards the latter, is a lesson that was innovative in its time and still today is of crucial importance, which we recommend not only in negotiation, but in any conflict situation. In adopting this behavioural and communicative strategy, on the other hand, and in addition to Fisher and Ury's suggestions, Dale Carnegie's authoritative teachings, to which we deem we should refer many times, will be very useful too.

Equally original and innovative is the emphasis that Harvard's method places on the real negotiating interests underlying the positions and therefore on the need for communication processes aimed at identifying and evaluating each other's interests. Indeed, it is on the latter that we must negotiate, and not on positions. *Getting to Yes* taught us not to stop at appearances, but to commit ourselves to get to the substance of things: that is what every good negotiator must actually learn to do.

On the other hand, we disagree with the absolute value that the method attributes to the other two inspiring principles. With regard to inventing options for mutual gain before deciding what to do, apart from the fact that the first and most important invention of multiple options likely to bring mutual benefits is that which every experienced negotiator should already provide in the preparation phase, it is not clear why, if the progress in negotiation allows it, it would not be appropriate to proceed immediately to take decisions that may emerge as in our favour.

Finally, as regards the use of so-called "objective criteria", this principle may be valid in negotiations on values or prices (e.g. in the sale of a used car) or balances between resources capable of objective technical evaluation (e.g. the characteristics of different weapons systems in a disarmament negotiation), but may not extend to general use. In fact, it should not be forgotten, as Fisher and Ury themselves point out, that in negotiation sensations and perceptions always prevail over the reality of things; that the value of each concession is always subjective and variable depending on who puts it forward or receives it; and that therefore an agreement can be reached on the basis of "objective criteria" only in the rare case that both parties have "made them subjective" by agreeing to adopt them as their own.

2.3. The psychological and cultural profile of the negotiator

"Good negotiators are not born, but you become one", says Henry Kissinger. What? Almost every author of texts on negotiation is usually induced to mention the theme of the ideal gifts and necessary skills to become a "good negotiator", both as an indication of a trend and on the basis of the author's own concept of the more or less collaborative or competitive nature of the negotiation process.

Thus, if in the 18th century, in times of deception, conspiracy and intrigue, de Callières or De Felice insisted on the need for strict discipline, strong emotional self-control, absolute discretion and patience, in more recent times of increased political and commercial relations and therefore greater social interaction, the severe repression of feelings and emotions gradually gives way to a "controlled loosening of control". And while even today the inexperienced negotiator is more impulsive and passionate, the experienced negotiator has instead learned to differentiate their own behaviour and emotions and is more skilled in creating a cooperative climate and exploring the counterparty's interests.

In our opinion, the basic requirements of the good negotiator, equally necessary in both collaborative and competitive situations, can be summarized as follows:

a) education and general culture (including, in international negotiations, historical, political, and economic and social knowledge of one's own country and that of the counterparty, and an excellent knowledge of at least one working language);

b) vocational education, general (depends on the type of profession carried out) and specific (good knowledge of the object of negotiation);

c) personal qualities of tact and discretion, flexibility, patience and dignity: in a word, innate skills of balance and moderation;

d) psychological preparation (on themselves and, if possible, on the counterparty), based on the three levels of approach of every human being to reality, "logical", "affective", and "instinctive", and therefore on the ability to manage as best as possible the rational, emotional, and passionate aspects that always occur during each negotiation;

e) technical preparation for the negotiation, supported by skills in communication, intellect, decision-making and expression, as well as the ability to work in a team, to take risks and to think clearly even under pressure.

Those who wish to become a good negotiator will benefit from the study of our subject and, instead of the petty knowledge of tactics and countermeasures, will acquire an instinctive aptitude for negotiation. But personal experience will certainly be even more useful, enriched by a constant capacity for self-analysis.

2.4. National and international negotiations: so-called "cross-cultural interactions"

In dealing with the requirements of the good negotiator, we have already seen that the in-depth knowledge of the historical, political, and economic and social reality of one's own country must always be accompanied by an equally good knowledge of the main aspects of the counterparty's country. This necessary requirement basically summarizes the theme of similarities and differences between national and international negotiations which, more than the place of negotiations, depend on the culture to which the subjects belong.

Of course, negotiating in one's own country is very often an advantage, similar to that which in some sports derives from playing at home: and this, in terms of logistical and organizational convenience (including the possibility of using one's own language and a more effective control of time), greater ease in the negotiator's contact with their superiors to speed up decision-making processes and refine choices and, last but not least, better management of the external consequences of the negotiation with interested third parties, press and public opinion.

But, regardless of the place of negotiation, problems and difficulties that characterize international negotiations compared to national ones (be they political-diplomatic or economic-trade negotiations), i.e. so-called "cross-cultural interactions", occur in the direct relationship between the parties or, rather, between the respective cultures. Whether it is therefore an issue of negotiating in one's own country or abroad, what is decisive is the personality (and psychological-cultural education) of the counterparty.

During an international negotiation, we come into contact with and experience the counterparty's cultural differences at all three levels of activity: rational, emotional, and passionate. So it is not just a question of penetrating the mind of the interlocutor to reconstruct their calculations and reasoning, but of being able to understand their entire cultural system, made up of ways and behaviours, social conventions, emotional reactions, visceral impulses, and values that are different from ours. On the one hand, therefore, uses and the mentality of different peoples and countries in the approach to interpersonal relationships, work habits, hierarchical-organizational schemes, negotiation management, decision-making processes and even the use of time are very often different. On the other hand, since negotiation is mainly communication, it is precisely in terms of communication, verbal and non-verbal, that the greatest difficulties can occur.

About verbal communication, it must be immediately said that, where there is a possibility for both parties to use with discreet mastery a third working language, this is certainly to be preferred over the use of interpreters, which makes the climate of negotiation much more detached and cold. Indeed, in addition to the further question of the relationship between the negotiators and their interpreters which, like any other interpersonal relationship, may suffer from greater or lesser empathy, misunderstandings or roughness of character, even the best interpreter will never be able to reproduce the tones and different nuances of the negotiator's voice.

Moreover, and unlike the translator who has their time to reflect or consult vocabularies, the interpreter must operate immediately and effectively: which always makes them not completely reliable, if you think about the fact that sometimes there are in a language words that are untranslatable in another or expressions that, if translated literally, lose their nuances or risk having a negative meaning (think, for example, of the well-known case of the radio interview with the then UN Secretary-General, Kurt Waldheim, who arrived in Tehran in 1980 to try to resolve the hostages crisis at the US Embassy, whose phrase "I have come as a *mediator* to seek a *compromise*" was translated without assessing that both words have a derogatory meaning in Persian, and unleashed the wrath of the crowd).

As for non-verbal communication (so-called body language), gestures, behaviours, uses or reactions, if habitual for a people, may instead be absent in other cultural systems or assume totally different and even offensive meanings (just think of the different ways of presenting, managing interpersonal distances or expressing approval or disappointment at the negotiating table).

Crucial, therefore, for the good international negotiator is the need to always avoid stereotypes or prejudices, and instead to open up to a genuine intercultural understanding, before, during, and after every negotiation.

2.5. Bilateral and multilateral negotiations: in particular, the EU negotiations

Whether national or international, it has been already said that, depending on the number of parties, negotiation can be "bilateral" (if there are two parties) or "multilateral" (if there are more than two). The latter, although with internal phases, procedures and dynamics partly similar to those of bilateral negotiation, takes place in a different context and has some particular characteristics to bear in mind.

First, in multilateral negotiations the parties do not negotiate freely between themselves, but under the direction of a subject who stands over them, always or only on that particular occasion, provided anyway with a power to steer, coordinate, and control "*super partes*". See several examples: the Premier in a Council of Ministers, the CEO on a Board of Directors, the Secretary-General of the International Organization which promoted the negotiation and hosts its conduct, the *ad hoc* Secretariat of an international Conference, and so on. Since many parties join the same negotiation, the statements by each of them of their positions or interests, of proposals or counter-proposals, and of the reasons for refusal or consent to a supposed collective solution, i.e. the central negotiation activity, must not be carried out through a direct and personal bilateral dialogue with each of the counterparties, but through a public presentation addressed at the same time to all parties to the negotiation. This presentation and any (but few!) subsequent statements, which can only be made from time to time and only after requesting and obtaining the floor from the Chairperson of the plenary assembly, should therefore be prepared in the clearest and most synthetic terms possible and with more general than personalized contents.

Secondly, even if in a multilateral negotiation, as in a bilateral one, the final goal is to reach an agreement, that agreement is not expressed in the preparation of a common bilateral paper, but is the result of a collective work and a decision, taken depending on the situation unanimously or by a majority, on a single text of agreement, generally prepared by the Secretariat of the Conference and intended, after national approvals and ratifications, to bind all contracting parties. For this reason too, requests for amendments to the text should be limited (except where a total alternative text may be submitted) and deal with changes considered essential, on pain of causing irritation and rejection by the other parties to the negotiation.

Finally, and of course also depending on the type of negotiation and its specific contents, the strategy to be followed by the negotiator in a multilateral negotiation is partially different from that of a bilateral negotiation. With very few exceptions (if unanimity is required and if it is deemed appropriate, the intransigent defence of certain positions may ultimately prove to be rewarding), it is absolutely essential not to be left "isolated". In multilateral negotiations, one can sometimes achieve one's own goals also by supporting proposals from others. If this is not possible, it is necessary to be able to join forces with other parties which have ideas or purposes similar to ours, through group understandings to be achieved by means of a patient and shrewd action of informal bilateral contacts, usually, during breaks between plenary meetings.

A particular category of multilateral negotiations is that of negotiations conducted by the European Union on behalf of its Member States with third States on matters transferred to EU competence, which, perhaps more correctly, should be defined as "multi-bilateral". Their basic difficulty happens almost always in the "pre-negotiation" phase (but it can also recur several times in the continuation of the negotiations) and pertains to the elaboration (by the EU Commission), as well as the discussion and approval (usually by the Member States), of the "negotiating mandate" which will bind the European Union negotiator as to the objectives to be pursued and strategies to be adopted.

Where, in fact, it is not possible to resolve the interests of the Member States in advance and these are completely different from each other, the EU must negotiate to satisfy them all cumulatively, conducting an extremely long and complex negotiation, and set – as they say – on the basis of the "all or nothing" principle (nothing is agreed until everything is agreed). It should be noted however that, fortunately, it is not very common for all Member States to have similar, substantial interests in the same EU negotiation, and that those barely involved are therefore more likely to accept even more modest results.

The above is just to give an idea of the difficulties which weigh down the preparation and conduct of the EU negotiations, complicated by the inevitable connections with the prior definition of similar negotiations (with Member States) within the EU itself. But it also explains what the real problems of the European Union negotiations are, namely the "*rigidity*" and the "*disclosure*" of the negotiating mandate.

On the first problem, the lack of the necessary flexibility stems from the fact that the mandate authorizing the opening of negotiation, binding on the Commission and its negotiators, is defined by the EU Council of Ministers at the end of a consensual decision-making process by the national Governments that is sometimes very long and laborious. Once approved, it remains unmodifiable for the Commission's delegation, which is forced to retrace the same process backwards whenever there is a need to readapt the strategy or to ask for new instructions.

With regard to the second problem, namely the need for the counterparty not to have precise knowledge of the extent of the concessions which the EU negotiator is in a position to make, it should be borne in mind that the content of the mandate is almost always the result of a public debate, so that the third State is aware not only of the limits set for the negotiation, but also of the different views expressed by individual Member States, and can get a clear idea of the deployment of forces within the EU and how to influence them.

2.6. Nature and specificity of diplomatic negotiations, and the so-called "diplomatic method"

General instrument of States' international relations, diplomatic negotiation, bilateral or multilateral, is first and foremost an "international" negotiation by definition, with the State itself as its subject and its diplomatic agents as negotiators. The latter are hierarchically dependent on the Minister for Foreign Affairs (from whom their instructions come), but in the receiving State, where they are accredited as Ambassadors, they functionally represent their Heads of State and public bodies as a whole.

With regard to possible issues, diplomatic negotiation ranges across the different aspects of the State's international activity: political, military, defence, security, economic, commercial, social, scientific, cultural, and so on.

For their better preparation and conduct, in all diplomatic negotiations the two parties make use of the close cooperation of their competent Embassies (as a rule, that of the sending State, accredited to the State that will host the negotiating round). The Embassy officially introduces (legitimizing it through a special "Note Verbale") the delegation that comes to negotiate at the local Ministry of Foreign Affairs and with the latter takes care of the organizational-logistical preparations of the negotiation.

Always on the subject of diplomacy, a very brief reference should be added to what, more in doctrine than in practice, is called the "*diplomatic method*".

More than a real method, it is in fact a value concept and a training criterion. Inspired by the similar principle of "good faith" that applies to the private discipline of contracts, the "diplomatic method" is, to use a beautiful and concise definition, "that way of conducting international relations that is based on negotiation and that tends to agreement"[50].

Seen from this angle, negotiation presents itself as the very essence of diplomacy, understood as the international activity of States: that difficult, but patient and unceasing activity, which alone is of use, if not in establishing a "positive peace" made up of "social justice and the absence of structural violence", at least in protecting the relative stability of a "negative peace", and the modest, but solid and reassuring, daily certainties for which every individual and every people aim.

---

50 Adolfo Maresca, *Dizionario giuridico diplomatico (Diplomatic legal dictionary)*, Giuffrè, Milan, 1991.

2.7. The "culture of negotiation": distinctive features, method, and values

Real and hard clashing-meeting of minds and characters, in a seesaw of controlled communication and patient exploration and analysis of interests concealed by the counterparty, and not speculative search for new organizational or socio-political models utopianly suitable to prevent any conflict. Constant effort at creativity and active imagination in the continuous options game and the ever-difficult exchange of concessions, and not generic strategies like *problem solving* (which is quite another thing, representing - as we have seen - in the "participatory management" known to the science of organizations a collective method of decision-making analysis similar to negotiation, but without the exchange of substantial concessions[51]). Not theoretical abstractness, therefore, but pragmatic concreteness: all this is today what we always love to define and illustrate as the "*culture of negotiation*", which it is worth here going through with some comments on its difference from other approaches and methods, characteristics, and values.

It is first and foremost evident that a "culture of negotiation", while intending to pursue at every opportunity and at all levels the peaceful resolution of disputes, should not be confused with those disciplines - such as the "*ethics of politics*" or "*peace studies*" - which aim to build an ideal and abstract society from which all forms of competition and struggle are banned. On the contrary, our subject is based on the assumption that conflict is inherent in any human system, realistically accepts its existence, analyses its causes and characteristics in the knowledge that not all conflicts are necessarily negative, and strives to prevent it from degenerating into open war, destroying resources and human lives, trying instead to control it

[51] D.A. Lax and J.K. Sebenius, *The Manager as Negotiator*, Harvard Negotiation Roundtable, 1986.

and channel it to a negotiating table (just as insidious but much less bloodthirsty!).

A "culture of negotiation", therefore, that is a much broader concept than American "*negotiation*" because, unlike the latter, it not only studies theories and techniques of negotiation, but also considers and analyses negotiation in all its facets. A focus on negotiation that obviously should not be understood as a "*sales technique*", let alone as a "*buying technique*" for, while it certainly contains elements specific to both[52], the culture of negotiation goes far beyond them, taking an interest in the more general aspects of any kind of conflict or process for settling interdependent disputes. This is how such a difference has been described by some French scholars (Guérin, Laborey and de Angéli): "Selling means inducing the customer to convince themselves that the proposed product or service best meets their needs. Negotiation, on the other hand, means analysing together a situation in which there is a common interest, in order to reach an agreement satisfactory to both"[53].

Considered as a difficult, but always stimulating and productive, path from conflict to consent, the culture of negotiation reveals a rich plurality of values.

First of all, it has an intrinsic "cultural" value, for the refinement of intelligence and sensitivity, for the stimulus to rationality, reflection, creativity, and the unexpressed potential of minds, for the development of interactions and synergies between individuals and peoples of different mentality, character, and culture.

---

[52] On the other hand, it is common practice during negotiations, at least in diplomatic jargon, to say to be committed to ensuring that the counterparty "buys" (or to have managed to "sell" to the counterparty) an idea, an operational concept, a particular wording, a goal, or whatever else it is hoped that the counterparty could share.

[53] Jean-Louis Guérin, Jean-François Laborey, Gérard de Angéli, *Formation à la vente*, Editions de l'Entreprise, Paris, 1979.

It reveals a high "social" value, as a suitable means to establish more effective interpersonal communication, to allow controlled vent to tensions, to create and spread tranquility and certainty, order and collective well-being.

It has its own specific "economic" value, resulting from increased possibilities for meeting needs, more efficient reallocation of resources, stimulus to inventiveness and productivity, creation of added value and, above all, cost savings of the conflict.

It has a significant "political" value, as a means of democratic search for consensus, for the peaceful overcoming of conflicts, for the maintenance of orderly civil coexistence, for security and stability, against war and violence.

In conclusion, it has a very high "ethical" value, as a means of developing the individual and enriching personality, deepening mutual knowledge, positively approaching interpersonal relationships, of education in understanding, tolerance, respect, and cooperation, against intimidation, blackmail, brute force, and subjugation.

All this is a "culture of negotiation". Expression of freedom (that freedom that Tacitus attributed to the parties to a negotiation, the sole architects of their right) and sense of responsibility (of the parties to a negotiation that are truly animated by "*voluntas negotiandi*" and "*voluntas concludendi*"), the culture of negotiation is the only keystone for the transformation of "understanding why" of a conflict: a why no longer addressed to the past (for what reasons? and whose responsibility?), but to the future (to what end have we supported a conflict? and what positive effects will its solution now have?).

Finally, it should not be underestimated that, while starting from a secular and utilitarian perspective, the culture of negotiation can also prove in practice a factor in the realization of that "*opus justitiae*" and "*tranquillitas ordinis*" and - why not? - even that "*opus caritatis*" which, according to St. Augustine and St. Thomas respectively, ultimately represents true peace.

Part Three

TECHNIQUE OF NEGOTIATION

3.1. Preliminary indications

Now that we have reached the third and final part of this Compendium, which focuses on the "negotiation technique", it is appropriate to start with some preliminary indications.

We have already taken the occasion to mention the very limited utility which, for a genuine understanding of the negotiating phenomenon and for its satisfactory theoretical and practical learning, the mnemonic study of petty rules of behaviour and minute tactics and countermeasures most often has. In addition to the intellectual dispersion it would cause, and the lack of adequate space and time here, such a study would have the same effect as those who felt that they had achieved full and reliable medical experience only on the basis of a small first aid manual!

Negotiation is always unpredictable, as are the conflicts of interest and the obscure objectives underlying it. And it cannot be addressed by looking each time for a specific suggestion for each of its different occurrences, as some kind of user's manual, which would risk distorting perceptions and altering judgment.

This is why we have considered it preferable to adopt a more general approach and an easier psychological-cultural synthesis, aimed at the formation of a kind of "behavioural and pragmatic self-consciousness", made up of a lowest common denominator of basic principles, that allows us to better recognize, analyse and manage behaviours, ambiguities, and uncertainties that accompany any kind of negotiation.

Then, since the theoretical and methodological part of our subject has been exhausted, we will now move on to illustrate a theoretical-practical synthesis of a typical bilateral negotiation process, where it will also be possible to find some information and guidance to deal with multilateral negotiation.

A theory shared by many authors, especially those belonging to the American school, divides the development of a standard negotiating process into six phases: preparation (so-called "pre-forming"), meeting and creating positive relations with the counterparty ("informing"), start of negotiations and progressive deepening ("forming"), confrontation and search for or offer of concessions ("storming"), reaching the understanding ("norming"or "performing"), conclusion and follow-up to the negotiation ("post-performing").

In the synthesis carried out in this book, we have preferred, while maintaining the useful pun of those definitions, to set out a different 4-step split, which seems to us to be more in line with the reality of the situation as perceived by negotiators. It must be borne in mind, however, that the negotiation process is always a continuum, in which the succession of phases is never so clearly detectable.

3.2. Phase I: Presentation (accreditation) and Preparation ("pre-forming")

Meaning by "*presentation*" that which normally precedes the first meeting between the parties and which is also valid as implicit "*accreditation*", it consists of an exchange of formal communications between the bodies to which the two negotiators belong. Most of the time the written communication is only that of the sending body, since the receiving one has already formally proposed at the time the opening of the negotiation or has merely taken note of the availability of the counterparty through ordinary communications or even through unofficial channels (that were, in the past, a phone call or personal communication; today nothing is more unofficial than an email!). This exchange of communications, besides containing names and qualifications of the negotiator and of all the members of any delegation of which they are the head, at the same time is of use in confirming also the place, date and time of the start of the negotiation.

There may be various types of presentation, more or less formal and more or less typical of different professional fields. With the exception of what was explained above, there are no proper binding rules in this regard. However, it is worth mentioning here the commercial practice and, above all, the diplomatic one, which both respond to more established usages and formalities.

In business practice, the exchange of communications between the two companies takes place by email or, in the most important cases, by letter, often delivered by hand. Since the communication of the appointed negotiator implicitly amounts to the attribution to the latter of the pertinent "negotiating capacity", this legitimation to the negotiation, which in some cases could also extend to the signing of the agreement, must necessarily come from a hierarchical superior of the negotiator (Chairman or Board of Directors for the Chief Executive Officer, the latter for the

Directors subordinate to him, a Director for a manager or an official below them, etc.).

More demanding and formal, since it concerns not private interests but the interests of States, is diplomatic practice, involving the Ministries of Foreign Affairs of the two parties and their respective Embassies. As a rule, the competence to define the terms of a diplomatic negotiation, agreeing all the logistical-administrative aspects, falls to the Ministry of the State that will receive the counterparty's Delegation, and the counterparty's Embassy. At the end of the consultative and decision-making process which, on the object, purpose and logistics of the negotiation to be undertaken, will have seen the competent offices of the Foreign Ministries engaged in the two capital cities, it is therefore the Embassy of the sending party that officially communicates to the receiving Ministry names and qualifications of the Head and all members of the Delegation, in addition to the date and time of their arrival, and the name of the same Embassy's official who will assist the Delegation.

This formal communication, which takes place through a "Note Verbale" (the written act by which official communications between a country's Foreign Ministry and the foreign Embassies accredited there take place) signed by the Ambassador or one of their delegates, performs also an implicit function of "accreditation" of the negotiator to the authorities of the receiving State to legitimize them for that specific negotiation. If, on the instructions of their own Ministry, the negotiator is the resident Ambassador and not a diplomat sent from the capital, they will not need any document that gives them the negotiating capacity, the latter being automatically included in their powers as Ambassador regularly accredited to the receiving State (on the contrary, the question of signature is different, for which, as we have already seen, even an Ambassador can only be legitimized through the "full powers" received from their own Minister).

Wrongly underestimated (either because of lack of time or because of a superficial conviction that it will be possible to do it once on location), the "*preparation*" is on the contrary a phase of basic importance and sometimes determines the whole negotiation process. Just think of the fact that this is the only phase in which the negotiator is still alone, without the pressure represented by the counterparty's presence, and in which they still have time to deepen the preparatory analysis of the issue under negotiation, obtaining further useful documentation and/or seeking further instructions from their superiors. Everything that has not been done during the preparation will have to be done on the spot, under much less favourable communication, logistical, and time conditions.

Once defined in good time relations with their own organization and with the members of their delegation, and clarified with their superiors any doubtful aspect of the received negotiating mandate (which will have to be, it is hoped, as flexible as possible), the wise negotiator will extend their preparation, from the analysis of the object of negotiation, to a general reflection on the conditions for the carrying out of the negotiation, to a prior assessment of the interests at stake, the objectives to be pursued and possible alternatives, to the characteristics of the counterparty (if known), to any precedents or possible side effects on other current or future negotiations, finally, to arrive at a broad approach to the strategy and tactics to be adopted.

This means, in particular, determining, as precisely as possible, what we want to achieve through negotiation, also identifying the "minimum" goal without obtaining which the negotiation will no longer be of interest (if "interest in negotiating" < BATNA). The other "negotiating interests" should then be graduated depending on their importance, in order to know clearly those that can be progressively conceded without excessive sacrifice when it will be necessary to make one or more concessions. And above all an in-depth reflection will have to be carried out on their own and the (conceivable) other's "negotiating power", looking for ways to strengthen the former and mitigate the latter: the ways, that is, in which to "hook the mind" of the counterparty not to "convince" it, but to "motivate" it.

To this end, the basic tool is the so-called "*argumentative list*", i.e. the list of possible arguments in support of one's own positions and those designed to counter the interlocutor's positions (if foreseeable), which the experienced negotiator will prepare, in the first place, bearing in mind the counterparty's interests that already appear manifestly decisive.

The negotiator who heads a delegation will also be able to carry out beforehand a greater or less substantial part of all the aforementioned preparatory work with the members of the delegation itself, both to deepen technical information in the possession of their experts, and to assign the most appropriate roles to the different members of the delegation, thus orchestrating in advance a better team game.

3.3. <u>Phase II: Meeting and establishment of positive relations with the counterparty</u> ("informing")

Finally, the time has come for the first meeting between the two negotiators and any respective delegations for the actual start of the negotiation. There are no special rules or techniques in this regard, not least because the different approaches or styles depend closely on the character of the negotiators, their psychological-behavioural upbringing and their ethical-professional preparation.

There are, however, a number of general criteria to which we should try to conform and which can be summarized as follows.

a) The first meeting consists, as always and everywhere, of a series of informal talks aimed at establishing or, if already pre-existing, deepening the interlocutors' mutual familiarity. But unlike what happens in everyday life, in the phase before each negotiation, more than just personal acquaintance, attention must be paid to a real analysis of the counterparty, their appearance, behaviour and character tendencies, external organization, relationship with the members of their delegation, their likely level of decision-making power and their apparent greater or lesser openness: all this, bearing in mind that, of course, the other side will do the same to you. It will therefore be necessary to always show a "façade" of openness, but without neglecting careful observation and "control".

b) It is known that the first impression is always (the most) important. Therefore, an additional criterion of the above to be borne in mind, is the opportunity to (help) establish a good atmosphere, in order to create with the counterparty (and what is true between the two negotiating Heads of Delegation is also valid between the individual members of both delegations) as positive interpersonal relationships as possible, which will often affect the progress of the whole negotiation. In order to do this, it is essential to avoid both excessively confident or closed attitudes, as well as long silences or hesitations. After the personal presentations (and do not forget to inform yourself first about the usages and customs of the receiving party), it is advisable to continue each conversation for a while, showing interest in your interlocutor and in what they are saying.

c) It should always be considered that peoples attach different levels of importance to the preliminary establishment of a good interpersonal relationship: citizens of Arab or Latin American countries, for example, do not start discussing business until at least a minimum of mutual knowledge and trust has been created between the parties and, unlike those from Anglo-Saxon or Central European cultures, allow a shortening of physical distances; on the contrary, negotiators from northern European countries are more inclined to reserve pleasantries and friendly conversations to the end of the negotiations and to maintain greater physical distance from the interlocutor; citizens of southern European countries consider it easier to establish positive relations during external social events, almost always convivial; and so on.

d) Both in informal conversations and even more so in official talks, at least at the initial stage of negotiations, it is always prudent to avoid controversial issues; while topics traditionally regarded as very sensitive (politics, religion, gender relations, etc.) can be accepted if we express our interest in information and learning, and not with questions that may sound critical or judgmental.

Finally, in order to complete an initial general assessment of the situation, we have to consider the importance of logistical and organizational issues and, in particular, the theme (which could also take on remarkable significance and consequences) of the seating arrangements at the "negotiating table".

It is up to the party hosting the negotiation (in a negotiation in several stages the hospitality is taken in turns) to provide for the logistical and organizational measures of the meeting. It should be considered that often these "protocol" aspects are not neutral, but they are used to signal to the counterparty the attention with which one looks at the results of the negotiation (all this without, however, formalizing too much and mistaking for rudeness a lack of attention that may simply depend on a different cultural tradition or, as between European countries, on the high frequency of meetings).

Once in the negotiation room, it is always advisable to report immediately to the host party, with due courtesy, any situation that may be of serious annoyance (uncomfortable chairs, sunlight in the eyes, air conditioning, etc.), so that it does not subsequently have to adversely affect the atmosphere of the negotiation.

With regard to the seating arrangements at the "negotiating table", in bilateral negotiation, delegations sit opposite each other. The two Heads of Delegation always take their place in the centre, usually behind a little flag of their own country which indicates, in this way, also on which side of the table to sit (as a rule, the host party with its back to the windows and the other with its back to the door), with the Delegation members alternating to their right and left. The more we want to stress the formal nature of the meeting, the more care will be taken to ensure that the seats are allocated according to the rank of each member. If the table is oval or elliptical and the two delegations are numerous, you may have them in contact at both extremes: which can sometimes favour a more friendly atmosphere and be of great use.

When there are more than two parties, the table takes the form of a polygon (with the same sides to emphasize the equal rank of all participants) or, most of the time, a circle. At a round negotiating table, which highlights even more the equal importance attributed to all delegations, each delegation may have one, two or (in rare cases) three seats at the table, while the rest of its members sit behind the Head of Delegation (in Italian diplomatic jargon: "they sit in aquarium", that is, keeping silent like fish!).

3.4. Phase III: Bargaining, progressive confrontation, and exchange of concessions ("forming" and "storming")

The phase of the "bargaining" (the term "negotiations" used in the plural refers rather to many successive rounds of negotiating) is the most complex, the most challenging and the most event-dense of the whole negotiation. Unlike the others, it also has a normally clearly visible start, because it coincides with the moment when the two delegations take their place at the negotiating table for the first time.

The first to speak is always the Head of the host delegation and, for each of the two parties, only the Heads of Delegation always speak, who are also the only ones that can authorize interventions by members of their own party. As in boxing matches, so in the most difficult negotiations, the first "round" is essentially of mutual study. The Head of Delegation of the host party renews their welcome to the delegation of the counterparty and, followed closely by their opposite number, introduces once again, this time formally and in hierarchical order, the other members of their delegation.

The two Heads of Delegation then move on to define the organizational arrangements for the conduct of the work and to discuss (or formally approve, if already agreed) the "*agenda*" of the work itself. In this respect, it should never be forgotten that the approval of the proposed agenda, always submitted by the host party, is never a foregone conclusion, since the counterparty can (indeed must) review it first with great attention, to verify the acceptability of the assumed order of priority of subsequent topics and to check that other issues or topics considered of fundamental interest are not missing.

The two Heads of Delegation then summarize, in an introductory speech, the negotiating "field", exchanging (but broadly and cautiously) the first information on what they intend to obtain from the negotiation. This is a very delicate step, for which there are no precise indications, since the attitude of the Head of Delegation may depend on many variables, first of all the assessment of the opposing negotiating tactics. If the interlocutor is known, because we have already had the opportunity to negotiate with them, it is generally productive to immediately put the "cards on the table", avoiding wasting energy on covert manoeuvres, remembering the progress already made together and identifying soon the areas of common interest.

But far more caution, on the contrary, is advisable if the interlocutor is new and unknown even if, in order to establish with them too from the beginning of the negotiation a good cooperative climate, you can use both the suggestions of the already described "Carnegie method" for managing interpersonal relationships and some specific techniques such as the following:

a) search immediately a number of positive answers on minor (e.g. procedural) issues on which it is almost certain that the counterparty will agree;

b) express yourself with a less direct and energetic language, often using the conditional ("I would like" instead of "I want", etc.), putting before proposals expressions of doubt ("perhaps", "I think that", etc.) or resorting to questions to make suggestions or proposals (essential with English-speaking interlocutors, for whom a direct style can sound aggressive);

c) carry out the "opening statements" in a clear and explicit way, to give the counterparty the opportunity to understand your needs and interests;

d) especially at the beginning, do not directly formulate assumptions about the interests of the counterparty, because it could be very irritating and harm a cooperative climate, but perhaps ask if your hypothesis is correct, repeating the counterparty's statement and asking if this really means what you have understood.

At the negotiating table, after the pleasant introductory rituals, the discussion and approval of the agenda, the first "opening statements" (always ambitious, provided they are sustainable!) and the first exchange of information on their respective positions, the bargaining gets underway with the presentation of one's own thesis ("argumentation"), the rebuttal of that of the other party (the environment heats up!), the discussion of the various options on the table (and the possible introduction of new ones), the formulation of proposals and counter-proposals, and questions and clarifications, the search for and exchange of concessions, and so on, until we very often reach "deadlock", when agreement seems increasingly difficult to achieve.

In order to effectively address the entire bargaining process in the single or subsequent "rounds" of which the negotiation consists, in addition to endeavouring to always keep people clearly separate from the problems and the apparent positions from the real basic interests (see the aforementioned "Fisher & Ury's method"), the following activities must be carefully taken into account and well used as instruments:

a) analysis of positions and arguments;
b) progressive exploration of interests, perceptions, and needs;
c) questioning technique;
d) active listening;
e) non-verbal language;
f) possible cognitive traps;
g) use of time.

On each of them books and books have been written, and still could be written. Since this, for reasons of space, is not the most suitable place to deal with them in depth, we will restrict the arguments to descriptive notes, short but complemented by useful operational indications.

a) The "*analysis of positions and arguments*" is the first form of logical and dialectical activity that is confronted at the beginning of bargaining. In principle, it is never appropriate to immediately challenge strongly arguments put forward by the counterparty in support of a position, since it is not on the positions that we should negotiate, but on the real interests that underlie them: to do the opposite would only risk irritating the counterparty and pushing it to become even more defensive, to the detriment of the necessary communication process and the identification of actual interests.

It should also be remembered that, especially in the bargaining activity, it is always clear to every experienced negotiator that "understanding" does not mean "agreeing". Therefore, unless you have valid (i.e. objective) arguments to offer immediately, which are equal and contrary, you can understand an argument of the counterparty as functional to its position, but without agreeing with it if its position is not acceptable, because based on needs and interests that still conflict with yours.

It is therefore essential to progressively deepen the identification and evaluation of the counterparty's real interests, by means of specific techniques.

b) Strictly integrated and interdependent on this activity is in fact the "*progressive exploration of interests, perceptions, and needs*". To achieve this it is useful to resort to Maslow's well-known theory of "pyramid of the 5 basic needs"[54], from which we learn that 60% of them (physiological, safety, and belonging needs) are instinctive, 40% (recognition and self-realization needs) affective, and none rational. From this theory, transposed by some scholars[55] in the so-called "list of 10 trade negotiation needs", we deduce that, not only for companies but for each individual, the needs that drive negotiation are 40% instinctive (needs to exist, security, comfort, and action), for another 40% affective (needs of solidarity,

[54] Abraham Harold Maslow, *Motivation and Personality*, Harper & Row, New York, 1954.

[55] Jean-Jacques Delage and Max Mayette, *Mieux négocier avec la grande distribution*, Chotard et Associés, Paris, 1986.

appearance, affectivity, and consideration) and only for the remaining 20% logical (needs of curiosity and economy).

So, according to this now widely agreed theory, in any negotiation only 20% of the activities are due to the sphere of rationality, against 80% to the one of irrationality, traceable back to the spheres of emotion (40%) and passion (40%).

c) The latter, fundamental remark must be taken into account in the use of the so-called "*questioning technique*", always very useful in bargaining, since well-formulated questions make it possible to drive the interview and deepen the knowledge of the real interests of the counterparty, sometimes "helping" it to clarify them better even to itself. Let us see below some basic rules:

- firstly, it has already been said that, in order to establish a good negotiating climate, it is advisable to immediately induce a series of positive answers on minor (e.g. procedural) issues on which it is almost certain that the counterparty will agree;

- between "open" questions (to which one can reply in different ways and by processing) and "closed" questions (to which one can answer with a "yes" or a "no", or with a very short answer), it is always preferable to formulate the former at the beginning of the bargaining, in order to stimulate wider communication exchanges, and the latter towards the end, to facilitate its conclusion;

- "open" questions, asked at the beginning, can also influence the interlocutor's opinions by inspiring new ideas; the "closed" ones are also of use, in the face of an interlocutor who speaks little, in stimulating at least some short answers and, in the face of those who speak a lot, in resuming the lines of discussion;

- in addition to obtaining information, questions are also useful to ensure you have correctly understood what the counterparty intended to communicate: if you have doubts, you should not talk, but ask questions;

- and finally, four common mistakes should be avoided, that is never ask: 1) more than one question at the same time (otherwise you risk receiving an answer only to the easiest one); 2) an alternative question (unless you are able to meet both options); 3) a rhetorical question that also contains the answer (it is useless and irritating); 4) a question that is actually a form of aggression (for the same obvious reasons)[56].

d) Of course, an effective questioning technique is not very useful without first carefully listening to what the counterparty has said. It is so-called "*active listening*", a technique similar to that of a psychoanalyst (or, if you like, of our best friend): it is not only listening carefully and showing interest in the counterparty, but also a technique of "suspension of judgment" and "stimulus" for the interlocutor to reflect and clarify their needs or interests. To be effective, it must not be superficial, but genuinely designed to understand other points of view. Nor should it give the impression to the counterparty that the intention is to "psychoanalyse" them or wants to make it a "third degree interrogation" and must always be accompanied by particular attention to the non-verbal reactions of our interlocutor.

Active listening reactions may consist of silence, nods of approval or encouragement, paraphrases or repetitions, or of trying to reinterpret what the other has expressed, or with questions that suggest one of our ideas by diverting the other from what they have said, until they can be confronted, but constructively, with inconsistencies or gaps in their way of thinking. Active listening should be used when there is a lack of crucial information on the needs of the counterparty and we feel that it does not have completely clear ideas and, above all, when taking a decision falls to our interlocutor.

On the contrary, it should never be used in the case of long periods of silence at the beginning of the bargaining, or when we

---

[56] For a brief but very effective illustration of the subject, see in particular: Vera F. Birkenbihl, *FrageTechnik, 19*, MVG, Munich, 1990.

have clearly understood the situation and, above all, when taking a decision falls to us, and the counterparty has taken that into account.

e) Reference has already been made to the importance of the so-called "*non-verbal language*" (or "body language") as it is able, if correctly interpreted in supplementing verbal language, to clarify unexpressed opinions and reveal intentions concealed by the other party. Of all the negotiating activities that take place during bargaining, non-verbal language is the one that attracts most curiosity and interest showing itself in multiple forms and that is therefore the matter of numerous texts and studies. It would be impossible here, for lack of space, to outline even the essential characteristics, so rich is the variety of gestures, positions, and behaviours, and their different motivations and countless keys to interpretation. However, some general indications can be given:

- the vast majority of the body's non-verbal signals are usually analysed by scholars in terms of attitudes of "openness" or "closure" (posture of the trunk, position of arms, hands, legs, etc.) or in "compensatory" terms of an inner discomfort, in the search for expressions of positive or negative feelings that could confirm or contrast verbal statements;
- psychological mechanisms from which non-verbal communication derives are very similar in all cultures, but each culture tends to process non-verbal messages differently; therefore the body language of the interlocutor must always be interpreted in its cultural context;
- in any case, non-verbal messages received from the counterparty must always be interpreted as a set of body gestures and in a general context;
- when analysing body language, it is always necessary to observe the details, but we should never judge what the interlocutor is thinking from a single gesture, which could be random and misleading;

- even if the other party does not understand body language, the positive gestures of one party usually lead the other to equally positive thoughts and gestures; and the same is the case with negative gestures;

- finally (and obviously!), never show the counterparty that you understand body language.

f) In the course of bargaining negotiators, while careful to pursue logical and rational processes, may, without realizing it, meet *possible "cognitive traps"* because the human mind, in assessing situations of risk and uncertainty, often tends to process the information received through "heuristics". The latter are very effective and intuitive cognitive procedures in terms of using and saving energy, but often responsible for so-called "cognitive distortions" (or "biases") in judgments and decisions, that we must be ready to recognize and neutralize. Below are some examples of the more frequent "traps", among those analysed by distinguished scholars of cognitive psychology[57]:

- "anchoring bias": in considering a decision there is a tendency to give disproportionate weight to the first information received; in bargaining the negotiators express their initial position and this remains for a long time an anchor that determines the perception of the possible outcome of the negotiations;

- "status quo": faced with two opposing alternatives, there is a tendency to save mental energy by passively choosing the status quo;

- "reactive devaluation": a value obtained from the counterparty is considered less desirable when it has granted it at its own initiative or too easily;

---

[57] Amos Tversky and Daniel Kahneman, *The Framing of Decisions and the Psychology of Choice*, in "*Science*", 211, 1981; and also: Max Hal Bazerman and Margaret Ann Neale, *Negotiating Rationally*, Free Press, New York, 1992.

- "sunk costs": there is a tendency to make choices that justify past decisions (investments), even if those decisions have proved to be wrong;

- "effect endowment" (i.e. "induced by possession"): it is difficult to give up something you already own in exchange for an asset of similar or even higher value (in bargaining, it is a different perception of the value of the concessions made compared to those received);

- "verification principle" (i.e. "confirmation of evidence"): we tend to search only for new information that confirms pre-existing beliefs, ignoring those that can contradict them.

The negative consequence of all these, and other, cognitive traps is the fact that, if not avoided, they lead to sub-optimal negotiating conduct, even in situations where much more satisfactory agreements could have been reached.

g) Finally, it is of crucial importance, especially in an international negotiation and if you are abroad, to know how to make good "*use of time*". In this regard, it should be borne in mind that the use of time is often a value varying from country to country, to a more rigid extent (for Anglo-Saxon cultures such as those of the United Kingdom, Germany, or the United States) or more flexible (for Mediterranean cultures such as those of Italy, Spain, Greece, or the Arab countries), faster (Western countries) or slower (Asian countries). A Western negotiator, for example, must therefore learn to be patient, whereas such a gift is practically innate in an Eastern negotiator.

In any case the passage of time puts both sides under pressure, adding stress to a situation that is already stressful in itself. For this reason, it would be appropriate to try to define with the counterparty, from the beginning, the time limits, intermediate and final, for the bargaining, in order to reduce, as far as possible, the emotional impact of the time factor. But this most of the time does not happen and, since the "deadline" may not be the same for the two parties, the one with the shorter deadline is subject to a greater pressure than the other to reach agreement and that element, if known, can be exploited.

The experienced negotiator knows that, while it would be desirable to proceed calmly, neither side agrees to make concessions too early. But it is often precisely the need to conclude by a certain date that prompts delegations to seek agreement more actively.

The last meeting is therefore the most difficult, it often takes place under conditions of considerable physical and mental fatigue for the negotiators and with less time to reflect on the others' proposals and to elaborate valid counter-proposals. The shrewd negotiator will try not to leave things to the very last, to a position of "take it or leave it", unless the alternative of "leaving it" is really possible: in this case the element of weakness can become a strong point, preventing the counterparty from dragging the bargaining along to ward off the (always delicate) moment of the final decision.

In agreeing on the timetable for the negotiations, it should not be forgotten that in a bargaining it is always necessary to be able to think with the necessary clarity: taking into account the consequences of jet lag and planning frequent breaks (also to tidy up ideas or consult with members of one's own delegation) are very useful measures, which the experienced negotiator must never overlook.

Let us now return to the progress of the bargaining, when both sides make more precise proposals and offers, always explaining the reasons before each proposal (if you make the proposal first, there is a risk that the counterparty will reflect on possible objections, instead of paying attention to your reasons), and continue (with different tactics and stratagems[58]) the stressful search for reciprocal and increasingly advantageous concessions. While reaching its "*climax*", the bargaining can often end in "dead-lock" and the agreement, instead of getting closer, seems impossible to achieve. In that case, and if further confidential confrontations, pauses or consultations between the two Heads of Delegation are fruitless, there is still a last special technique which aims to facilitate the overcoming of the "*impasse*" and the return to a more constructive and cooperative climate, useful for reaching agreement.

It is so-called "*brainstorming*", a method more than a technique that, in order to be effective, must respond to the following rules of conduct:

- first of all, it is stated openly, agreeing that an attempt will be made between the two parties on brainstorming;
- the two Heads of Delegation, each assisted by no more than two or three collaborators, meet informally, better in another room, and agree that nothing that will be said or written during the brainstorming will have any formal value;
- therefore, the small group of negotiators begins to generate ideas and options, as various as possible, including incongruous ones, triggering an imaginative process and, above all, suspending all judgment on the acceptability or refusal of the emerging proposals;
- once this process has been completed, the group then moves on to the (short) phase of an initial assessment of all the options formulated, only to exclude those deemed too abstruse or unacceptable and to focus instead on those to be brought back to the negotiating table.

[58] For a stimulating intercultural perspective on about 80 tactics preferred by managers from 11 different countries, see: D.W. Hendon and R. A. Hendon, *How to Negotiate Worldwide. A Practical Handbook*, Gower, Aldershot, 1989.

3.5. Phase IV: Understanding, conclusion of the Agreement, and follow-up to the negotiation ("performing" and "post-performing")

Once the impasse has been overcome, thanks to (or without) brainstorming, the two parties face the final phase of the negotiation, characterized by a sensitive (and evident) approach to the area of consensus and the achievement of understanding. At this stage, it is of crucial importance to ensure the increasing involvement of the counterparty to whom, if necessary, signs of recognition and appreciation for their "decisive contribution" to the solution of the common problem should be given even beyond their due. Careful observation of non-verbal language, closed questions, strict logic, kind but assertive tones, and renewed decision-making speed: everything is now resorted to, with what some authors call the "funnel technique"[59], in order to avoid the reopening of further matters and to close the bargaining once and for all.

At the end of it, the parties make a detailed summary of what has been said and recapitulate the understandings reached on the various points, the distribution of implementing responsibilities, any issues that remain to be clarified (if some points have been agreed only *ad referendum*, in order to submit them for approval by the respective superordinate authorities, they shall be written in square brackets), and any subsequent fulfillment.

Then, they move on to the careful joint review of the final text of the understanding (agreement or contract), its "*initialing*" in order to authenticate its final content with the initials of the two Heads of Delegation on the respective side margins of each page and, if they have the pertinent legitimation ("full powers"), also its official signature.

---

[59] John Ilich, *Dealbreakers & Breakthroughs*, John Wiley & Sons, New York, 1992.

A serious exception is when, on the contrary, due to unacceptable requests for excessive concessions it has not been possible to conclude the agreement. In this case, and having assessed the general situation and any possible alternative, it will still be extremely important and significant to conclude either a partial understanding or, at the very least, a so-called "*agreement to disagree*", which highlights the points (and underlying reasons) of persistent divergences. As mentioned in the first part, the agreement to disagree is a rather unusual act and almost always drafted in the form of minutes of what happened during the negotiation. It is very useful not only to highlight by consensus points and grounds for divergence thus establishing a basis for a possible and subsequent round of negotiations, but also to safeguard a positive relationship between the parties and to allow the negotiators themselves to report at least a minimum concrete result to their principals, "saving face" also in front of the media and public opinion.

The happy conclusion of each negotiation always creates very positive emotional and interpersonal effects between the negotiators. Especially if the agreement reached has resolved the issues on the table with fairness and to their mutual satisfaction, the relationship with the counterparty becomes consolidated also in the awareness of the "common victory" over the issue negotiated. And it becomes a source of possible, new and even more positive developments in the future.

All the more so, in this case, the negotiators return to their respective bodies with the implicit commitment to the verification of the operational follow-up to the agreement, starting by promoting and following, obviously within the limits of their competences, its ratification process and the beginning of subsequent implementation.

Conclusion

We now know that negotiation activity has always been an integral part of our nature and that, thanks to it, we can positively resolve the conflicts we are facing or achieve what we need but do not have, peacefully and constructively. Yet the idea of having to negotiate arouses anxiety and fear, because we are not used to managing conflicts. Of course, one of our limitations is that every time we get into a conflict we have a reading of the facts that is already a diagnosis. And instead, the initial step would be precisely to suspend judgment and arrive at a "non-judgmental vision" of the situation, to open our mind to objective analysis and understanding of the situation itself and of what caused it.

It is very difficult to keep under control our instinctive reactions of aggression and resentment, especially when we feel we are the target of others' aggression and resentment. If at that moment we could stop in order to listen to the voice of our mind and not that of our gut, to discuss peacefully with the "great intellectual enigma" and "emotional challenge" represented by the other, perhaps we would also win another more difficult battle, that with ourselves, to escape unscathed any conflict in the direction of true peace. Let us never forget that the inability to manage a conflict generates violence and that from confrontation to conflict, resentment, violence, and war, is but a short step. And presages the destruction of our own and other people's resources.

Perhaps the scholar or reader who has followed us so far, in the future, will have only a few memories of this discipline. We will be pleased if this has happened because learning will have been replaced by that instinctive "culture of negotiation" to which we have devoted our efforts.

Gustave Flaubert wrote in the mid-1800s: “You will not have what you want. You will get what you negotiated”. Learning to negotiate means learning to bend positive events in our favour and to modify negative ones, but not only this.

A well-known and very ancient prayer says: “Lord, give me the strength to change the things I can change and the patience to accept those that I cannot change, and wisdom to distinguish the difference between them.”

Strength, patience, and wisdom: yet, this culture of negotiation will perhaps help us achieve all three.

*   *   *   *   *

www.ingramcontent.com/pod-product-compliance
Ingram Content Group UK Ltd.
Pitfield, Milton Keynes, MK11 3LW, UK
UKHW042010190726
13854UKWH00005B/2232

9 781716 084423